IAN FLEMING:

MAN WITH THE GOLDEN PEN

IAN FLEMING:
MAN WITH THE GOLDEN PEN

© Copyright 1966 by
Swan Publishing Co., Inc.
All Rights Reserved.

DEDICATION

To Brian and Bob

IAN FLEMING:

MAN WITH THE GOLDEN PEN

*The following James Bond novels
are published by PAN Books*

CASINO ROYALE

LIVE AND LET DIE

MOONRAKER

DIAMONDS ARE FOREVER

FROM RUSSIA, WITH LOVE

DR. NO
GOLDFINGER

FOR YOUR EYES ONLY

THUNDERBALL

Also available

THE DIAMOND SMUGGLERS

THRILLING CITIES

The following are available in Signet Books published by The New American Library

CASINO ROYALE

DIAMONDS ARE FOREVER

DR. NO

FOR YOUR EYES ONLY

FROM RUSSIA, WITH LOVE

GOLDFINGER

LIVE AND LET DIE

MOONRAKER

ON HER MAJESTY'S SECRET SERVICE

THUNDERBALL

YOU ONLY LIVE TWICE

THRILLING CITIES

007 JAMES BOND: A report by O. F. SNELLING

—*ADDITIONAL BIBLIOGRAPHY*

— THE JAMES BOND DOSSIER
By Kingsley Amis
1965 By Jonathon Cape

— IAN FLEMING — THE SPY WHO CAME IN WITH THE GOLD
By Henry A. Zeiger
1965 By Duell, Sloan and Pearce

— DOUBLE O SEVEN — JAMES BOND: A report
By O. F. Snelling
1964 By Spearman-Holland Press

The authors wish to acknowledge the assistance
of the following:

Dr. Donald McCulloch

Dr. Stephen Neiger

Dr. John Rich

Dr. Betty Steiner

and

Connie Douglass, Bruce and Pat Fortnum, Brian and
Margaret Hogan, Ian Patterson, Norm Perry,
Lee Roach, Bruce and Eleanor Sabsay.

and

The Pierre Berton Show

About the authors

The twain did meet. While Eleanor was attending school in Regina, Dennis was cutting his writing teeth as a one-man night staff at the Dartmouth Bureau of the Halifax Herald and Mail.

Before they met, Eleanor earned her spurs as secretary of the Regina CCF, at age 17, union worker, held various jobs in film and television production and as a writer, public relations practitioner, editor and publisher.

Dennis returned to Canada after serving with the RCAF overseas to become a civil servant until boredom pushed him into freelance writing. This led inevitably to editing, public relations and more freelance writing.

They now enjoy the role of husband-wife writing team and the company of two large, good looking teen age sons and a juvenile German Shepherd. The sons were his wedding gift to her, the deranged dog was imposed on both of them.

The Pelrines enjoy life on "the wrong side of the tracks" just outside Forest Hill Village, share an office on the third floor of their "broken down duplex", enjoy life immensely and love to write when they are not busy doing more important things like riding their bicycles, entertaining, kibitzing with their boys and enjoying the fact that the twain did meet.

INTRODUCTION

James Bond, termed everyman's dream by one of his enthusiastic fans, does everything well. As the avenging angel, licensed to kill, he effortlessly disposes of villains. As the tastefully clad, discriminating smoker, drinker and eater, he moves effortlessly through the best clubs, gambles at the best casinos, and equally effortlessly, cleans up.

As a connisseur of fine cars with purring motors, he pilots them round hair pin curves, with the enemy in hot pursuit. As a superb athlete, he moves gracefully and excels at underwater swimming, golf, or any other game he might attempt.

Each approach to each tall, athletic Bond-girl with the sun-streaked hair is sure-fire. Bond is not only never rejected, he's never too tired or too busy . . . and the Bond-girls are never cold.

Ian Fleming's James Bond formula was sure fire, too — with disarming honesty, the author himself described it as "bang-bang, kiss-kiss!"

Fleming's 13 books, 4 of them translated to film, brought him almost three million dollars until his death in August, 1964. Translated into 11 languages, 12 of the books grossed 60 million dollars (the thirteenth, Man With the Golden Gun was completed and printed after Fleming's death.).

Countless James Bond and 007 merchandising gimmicks have been developed, and now constitute a multi-million dollar international enterprise. Sean Connery, the film James Bond, continues his relentless prowl, ferreting out international villains, and felling willing Bond-girls.

The British Government Estate Office is still, almost two years after the death of Fleming, pondering the succession duties to be charged his estate. Fleming's widow has been quoted as estimating that another three or four years will elapse before the estate is finally settled — even imperturbable British civil servants boggle at calculating the total value of his estate — with the dollars still pouring in.

Our objective: A cool, dispassionate look at Ian Fleming and James Bond — at Ian Fleming as James Bond, and at those hundreds of thousands of Bond fans, in such illustrious company as the late president John F. Kennedy, Prince Philip, Duke of Edinburgh, and CIA chief Allan B. Dulles, who couldn't wait for the next book and still go on talking about the last one.

CHAPTER 1

Ian Fleming, The Boy

Ian Fleming, born May 28, 1908 seems always to have been interested in heroes. The second of four sons of Major Valentine Fleming, member of parliament and distinguished soldier and the beautiful Evelyn Fleming, took his father as his first hero. The major was killed during shelling at Somme, France, on May 20, 1917, when young Ian was just eight.

There is little doubt that the boy Ian, deprived of a father's love and attention at a crucial early age, idealized the Major; or that Valentine Fleming, posthumously awarded the DSO, was a genuine hero. The Times of London, November 10, 1917, estimated the gross value of his estate at 265,595 pounds—over a million dollars.

Besides this legacy to his family, Major Fleming left the impressionable young Ian the ideal of service and duty by which he had lived.

The considerable wealth and social position enjoyed by the Fleming clan and Ian's maternal grandfather meant that Ian was never deprived, in a material sense. His early environment had a kind of Edwardian elegance, one Fleming later called "overprivileged", but Ian was grossly underprivileged, as far as parental affection and approval were concerned.

His beautiful mother, faced with the task of carrying on alone as head of the family was a harsh mistress, demanding of herself, and demanding of her children. Apparently she frequently made unfavorable comparisons between Ian and his older brother Peter, whose school performance was eminently satisfactory, and who later attained fame, in a socially acceptable way, as writer of several widely read and respectable books.

As a young boy, Ian Fleming was shipped off to attend Eton, described by writer Geoffrey Bocca in the Saturday Evening Post, as "an especially tough school, which specialized in beating conformity into young children.

Robert Harlach, quoted in the Spy Who Came In With the Gold, commented on spartan English treatment of young boys: "The English upper crust wants and needs affection as deeply as any other crust, but impulses toward this important emotional release are frequently stifled for them at about the age of eight, when boys go away to boarding school. Affection by letter and postcard is as broken-backed as most other emotions by proxy. The boys grow up, professing to hate what they so need. Hence the undertones of sadism and masochism so frequent among British males. Hence perhaps, those passages in the Bond books which have provoked such bitter attacks."

And certainly, Ian Fleming the boy, had his brush with the beginnings of sadism and masochism. At Eton, where he followed in the footsteps of his father and older brother, he felt that the Flemings were not especially well regarded.

He drove himself, far beyond normal endurance to become an outstanding athlete and was twice named Victor Ludorum or decathlon champion, winning every athletic event except the high jump, before he was sixteen. Combined with that stamina and keen sense of competition, Fleming frequently indicated high spirits, and was frequently slapped down.

Paul Gallico, who revisited Eton with Fleming, by then a successful author, recalls one especially painful episode when the young Fleming, having accumulated a disconcerting number of misdemeanors, was caned just prior to an important race. After the punishment, Fleming insisted on running, and finished second, although the blood streamed down the back of his legs. Concluded Gallico "Ian had one of the stiffest upper lips I have ever encountered upon any of my English friends. He was a courageous man.

Psychiatrists consulted on this point indicate that, to their knowledge, British public school floggings are rarely severe enough to open streaming wounds. What is significant, they contend, is that Fleming told this story, perhaps combining bitter reality and masochistic fantasy — not surprising, considering the rigorous, affection starved life of the English public school boy.

Fleming, anyone who has researched him will agree, never suffered from the writer's characteristic exhibitionism. Not only did he never bleed publicly about his childhood, he was reluctant to discuss many early experiences, and with appropriate British reserve, the members of his immediate family followed the same policy.

Not just an exceptional athlete, as a boy Ian Fleming displayed the first flashes of great intellectual curiosity, the same curiosity which was so useful in researching and documenting the Bond books.

Fleming's public school career was like many others in his generation and class. Even the homosexual initiation to which he occasionally referred in later years was regarded as par for the course. He was ambivalent about Eton and the public school system, feeling that it was probably an unnecessary ordeal, but enjoying a certain pride at having endured the experience, which had undoubtedly strengthened his character, or else what was it all about?"

Deprived in some respects, overly indulged in others, Ian Fleming was British through and through. Later, when he wrote of James Bond — and the villains who beset him — that became significantly apparent. The villains were never British — the more obscure and unlikely the racial origin Fleming could construct for them, the better.

Fleming made at least one fast friend at Eton. William Plomer, there at the same time, later helped the Bond creator edit the spy thrillers. According to the author's wife, Plomer was probably responsible for initiating Bond's gourmet kick — after he discovered that in an early draft, the secret agent seemed to be subsisting wholly on a diet of scrambled eggs.

After Eton, Fleming went on to Sandhurst, the British West Point, rather than to Oxford where his older brother Peter had enjoyed a brilliant career as a student at Christ Church College. Peter was president of the Oxford University Dramatic Society, an editor of Isis, the student literary magazine, and received a first in English.

Probably Ian chose Sandhurst because he was weary of tales of his brother's prowess.

At Sandhurst, Ian received a commission to a calvary regiment, and displaying a fondness for England's Edwardian past, turned it down, as biographer Zeiger says "because they were mechanizing the Army, and a lot of us decided that we didn't want to be garage hands running those bloody tanks."

An interesting point, which echoes the "snobbery" of the Bond novels.

Certainly, the young Fleming was closely tied to his mother, whose firm hand on his destiny cropped up over and over. His decision to drop out of the army, because he couldn't bear it, infuriated her, and she insisted that he do something respectable, and once again compared him unfavorably with his brothers who were all doing "splendidly".

In a move to please her, Ian chose to try for the Foreign Service, and went abroad to study languages at the University of Geneva and the University of Munich. He learned to speak and write fluent French and German, and acquired that dash of Russian which cropped up later in the Bond books. Fleming evidently felt that his two years in Germany and Switzerland were the most important part of his education, while things he had learned at Eton and Sandhurst vanished quickly.

After his study abroad, Ian returned to England in 1931 to write the Foreign Service examination. Again, he didn't quite make it, finishing seventh, in a competition for five openings. England was in the grip of the depression, and Ian, apart from his studies at a number of different schools, and collecting books, had done nothing to recommend him for employment anywhere.

He wrote a friend of his mother's, Sir Roderick Jones, then chairman of Reuters, enclosing a letter of recommendation from a mutual acquaintance.

Ian's letter, quoted in the "Spy Who Came In With the Gold" is as follows:

"Dear Sir Roderick,
I don't expect you will remember me, although we did once meet at a party here. I hope you won't think me presumptuous taking advantage of your friendship with my mother in order to write to you personally. My object in doing so, is, briefly as follows.

I have just taken the Foreign Office exam and passed adequately, but not brilliantly. In the normal course of events, I should try again, but I have decided not to, as I am really longing to start regular work as soon as possible.

My education has been 'international' above all else — Eton-Munich University — Geneva University — Hautes Etudes Internationales at Geneva and various minor institutions such as the "Foyer de Etudes Slaves" at Paris, etc. My languages are essentially practical, i.e. conversational, yet in the F. O. exam, I got 70% for both French and German and 56% for Russian. I have a good knowledge of Psychology and a Swiss 'certificate' in Anthropology. I worked for the Austrian government in the Secretariat of the League of Nations (sections for Intellectual Cooperation) and have translated one book and several articles from the German.

I have mentioned these facts in order to give you a vague idea of my capabilities and interests, and in the hope that you might consider the possibility of my being of use to Reuters. I have been given an idea of the work at Reuters, and I can only say that there is no profession I should prefer or to which I should devote myself with so much enthusiasm.

These are vain words and I should very much like to come and see you, if you think there is any chance of my getting into Reuters. Could you spare me a moment any day early next week?"

These are hard times and I expect you are chary of engaging any new staff. I shall be all the more grateful should you decide to take me on.

Yours sincerely,
Ian Fleming"

The letter of recommendation enclosed gives an indication of the circles in which the Fleming family moved, and the assistance he could muster when seeking a "suitable job".

"Dear Sir:

With reference to the enclosed I beg to say that I have known Mr. Ian Fleming all his life. His parents and grandparents have been my intimate friends for many years.

His grandfather is one of the most able, best known and highly respected men of business in the City of London, and his father, M. P. for South Oxfordshire, was a man of outstanding qualities.

He has therefore been brought up in surroundings where he has had the advantage of being associated with culture, practical business experience and knowledge of the world. He is personally a young man of great intelligence, energy and promise, thoroughly well educated.

He has been employed at the League of Nations Council; and I have heard the most satisfactory accounts of the impression made by him there. He has an excellent brain, and very good manners. He is quick and extremely intelligent. I can highly recommend him in every respect.

He should have a distinct career before him.

Yours faithfully,
Robert White

Such a commendation of Fleming's family and general breeding, while it might not be considered relevant to employment in North America, was undoubtedly effective at the time in Britain. But, because the English newspaper world is a rough one, the public school old boys fraternity was not the only factor to be considered. Editors were interested in recruiting men who could nose out the story first, in preference to those with the right accent.

Fleming had presented himself at just the right time, though. Sir Roderick was trying, says Zeiger, to improve Reuter's position in relation to the American competition, and believed that a few public school boys on staff might improve the tone of the service's dispatched. So, Fleming got the job, and his mother sent the proper letter of thanks to Sir Roderick.

"My dear Sir Roderick,

I am so glad to hear that you are giving Ian a trial. I am disappointed in a way that he is not having another try for the F. O. exam, as we never expected him to get in this year. However, I am delighted that he passed the exam, and if you find him useful it may be all for the best! He has great character and is supposed to be very intelligent, though I ought not to say so! I am just back

and hope to see you and Enid soon.
                              Yours v. sincerely."

Reading between the lines, it seems obvious that Mrs. Fleming's first reaction was one of relief that at last Ian had done something "suitable". Notice her reference "he is supposed to be very intelligent", evidently in her eyes, he suffered by comparison with his father and older brothers.

Despite the fact that stimulus for his employment had been personal and social, young Fleming shaped up and acquitted himself admirably. Memos of the period from his supervisor, Bernard Rickatson Hatt, to Sir Roderick, indicate that he was closely observed, and that Sir Roderick interested himself in Ian's development.

During his first month's probationary period, Fleming proved himself to be a worker. The same attention to detail which lent authenticity to the Bond books in his later life, won Fleming the attention and approval of his superiors and coworkers.

After a year of diligence, Fleming was convinced that he definitely had something to offer the Fourth Estate, and he wrote to Sir Roderick Jones, requesting that his salary, a nominal 150 pounds, be doubled.

Says Zeiger, in TSWCIWTG, "he told Sir Roderick that he was delighted with his work and enthusiastic about the whole organization, but that the day is past when a career is merely a hobby. He added that he had been for twenty-four years from the financial point of view *at least* (ITALICS OURS) "a dead loss to my family," and that he considered it his duty to start earning a living.

His family after inheriting the estate of more than a million dollars left by his father could hardly have been considered in difficult straits but the same lack of confidence in himself — which manifested itself in Fleming's later life, combined with the necessity to "prove something" to the disapproving mother, drove him to push for the raise.

Fleming went on to say that he regarded his first year with Reuters as training, and knew that the firm had made a substantial investment in him.

He wanted to know whether the management thought he had a future with Reuters, because he had received an offer from the banking firm of Robert Fleming and Co. Certainly Ian wanted to stay with Reuters and considered the banking opening unsuitable for his aptitudes and hopes for the future.

"But," quotes Zeiger, "I know you will appreciate the fact that I owe to my family and to myelf to assure my future as far as possible." Surely the young Fleming, with creative ability found the drive to ensure future security in conflict with his own preferences.

The answer to Fleming's polite ultimatum was a raise, in two stages, and Zeiger's book quotes Sir Roderick's note to the chief accountant saying that "a definite exception is being made for him because of the special circumstances of his case" . . . evidently that he could easily get another job paying more money, and that Reuters wanted to protect their investment in his training.

During his apprenticeship at Reuters, Zeiger says, he learned the tricks of his trade by rewriting advance obits and performing the other unexciting jobs which fall to the juniors in any news agency. He proved himself to be capable, and was well respected by his contemporaries and his elders. Alaric Jacob, who started with him on Fleet Street, recalled for Zeiger "Such good judges as Harold Nicholson and Robert Van Sittart predicted great things for Ian Fleming. He was not at the start a brilliant journalist:: o:thers of our circle progressed much faster than he, but behind Ian's languid good looks, the canny Scots way he had of deploying his talents, and his delightful capacity for friendship many people detected a glittering potential."

In the spring of 1933, Fleming snagged his first important assignment and made his first venture into the never-never land of darkness, secrecy lies and truth which he later wove into the durable and glittering fabric of the Bond books.

On March 13, 1933, the Times of London reported: "BRITISH SUBJECTS ARRESTED, ACTION BY OGPU IN MOSCOW." The story recounted that Alan Monkhouse, W. H. Thornton, John Cushny and W. H. Macdonald, employees of the Metro-Vickers Company of Manchester, had been arrested by the secret police, along with a Latvian and four Russians who worked for the same company. Monkhouse was taken by about half a dozen OGPU men, who surrounded his house while he was eating dinner. The company's offices were raided and their records confiscated. Later, two more British subjects, A. W. Gregory and C. de Nordwall were arrested on the same charge.

The arrests were a mystery in England. All the men charged were engineers, working on Russian construction projects. George Bailey, general manager of Metro-Vickers, told the Times:

"The news has come as a big surprise to the company. We have considerable commercial interests in Russia, where we are engaged in construction work, and the four men whose arrests are reported are four of our senior men in the country. They were engaged in an advisory capacity, and I am quite confident that neither they, nor any member of the company in Russia have done anything that would be contrary to Russian policy. We are sure that some mistake has been made and we are taking every measure we can to safeguard the interests both of the men and of the company."

Early reports in the English newspapers were shocked and naive. Speculative statements about the nature of the crimes allegedly committed were produced. Only gradually did British newsmen, steeped in traditions of British justice consider the possibility that no offence had been committed and guilt or innocence didn't matter.

In these first days of speculation, Fleming wrote a story, published with a Riga dateline, saying that the men would be charged with espionage in connection with the construction of the Dnieprostroy Dam. Specifically, Fleming speculated that the men were to be accused of corroding the blades of the turbines of the dam with malicious intent.

Fleming's story, the first specific information on the nature of the charges created a furor, and got Fleming into difficulty. The BBC picked up the story, without contacting Metro-Vickers before carrying it. The company issued several denials, and wound up by expressing the hope that "the company is still confident that the whole affair is a terrible mistake and that all the employees there under arrest ought to be released at once."

Fleming, meanwhile, had to report to Rickatson-Hatt on the way in which he had gathered the information.

His only crime seemed to be, that he had received it from a friend who was employed in the Vickers complex ... as a confidence, and not for publication. Tass, the Russian News Bureau, did not, for once, deny the Riga story ... lending credence to the idea that the engineers were to be charged as speculated by Fleming.

As the time for the trial moved nearer, it became apparent to Reuters management that it would be unwise to assign their regular Moscow correspondent to the case ... since the English press would have to be critical of Russia in reporting the case, and the regular bureau man who dealt with government officials almost daily, would be under tremendous pressure in that situation.

Fleming, handling reports of the lengthy and confusing trial for Reuters, contributed a great deal to the Western World's understanding of the Soviet government. His research and documentation of the "secret police" aspect of the proceedings was impressive, and during his assignment in Moscow he learned that British justice, with its principle of innocence presumed until guilt proven is by no means worldwide. Later, as author of the Bond books, he was to become expert in the examination of a moral — or amoral — code, foreign to his upbringing.

His factual reports of the trial and verdict prompted the competition, INS to cable Sir Roderick, commending Fleming's demeanour and handling of the story.

In fall, 1933, probably in reward for his performance, Ian received an offer from Reuters, to become assistant general manager in the Far East, at an annual salary of 800 pounds.

Considering that his salary at that time was just 300 pounds, the offer was not unattractive, but after taking time to think about it, Fleming rejected it. He later explained "because I knew I wouldn't be able to keep up with the Joneses of Singapore . . . it seemed to me that if the best position Reuters could offer wasn't going to bring in enough money, the only thing I could do was resign."

Once again the heavy, relentless, hand of Evelyn Fleming had pushed Ian into an action he didn't want and didn't need.

Henry A. Zeiger, in Ian Fleming the Spy Who Came In With the Gold, quotes two of Fleming's letters, one to Sir Roderick Jones, and the other to Rickatson Hatt, which was more revealing.

To Sir Roderick, he wrote:

"Just a week after our conversation, when I was about to write and accept the post you offered me, a businessman with whom I am only slightly acquainted asked me to see him and offered me what at first sight appeared to be a quite exceptional post in his firm of merchant bankers. The gist of the offer was that he himself intended shortly to retire and that he offered me his partnership in the firm after two years of learning the business.

Although the offer appeared too good to be true, I subsequently found that it was perfectly sincere and that the firm in question was one of the most successful and reliable in the city. A partnership would be quite remarkably remunerative and I would acquire before I was 30 a position which it is unusual to obtain before the age of 50, if at all.

Robert Fleming (his banker grandfather) and a director of Baring Brothers both urged me to accept the offer and, having regard to its quite exceptional nature and to the fact that it has been made in all sincerity, I am afraid that I have no alternative but to ask you to be kind enough to accept my resignation from Reuters."

The personal note to Rickatson-Hatt was:

"I enclose a copy of a letter I have just written to Sir Roderick. I can't say how sorry I am to have to take this step and I can hardly bear the thought of leaving Reuters after the wonderful two years training you have given me. I really had hoped to make a big career in journalism after all the encouragement you have given me, and the idea of having to go and sit on an office stool for the rest of my life is all the worse compared with the marvellous time you have given me with Reuters. But however much I hate the idea, I really can't afford to miss this amazing offer which will mean a hell of a lot of money very soon. It's a beastly idea giving up all the fun of life for money, but I hope I shall be able to make a packet and then get out and come back into journalism from the other end. Anyway, the decision had to be made, and I was pretty well pushed into it from all sides. I was assured it was the "right thing to do" for the sake of the family — so there it is.

I loathe the idea from nearly every point of view, and I shall hate leaving you and Reuters. But I'm afraid it has got to be done.

Please forgive me for repaying all your kindness and the wonderful two years you have given me in this rotten way."

Ian Fleming, at 25, rankled under the domination of mother, family and "respectability," but wasn't yet strong enough to throw off the yoke.

In later years, he spoke gratefully of his Reuters experience, explaniing that it was in Reuters that he learned to write quickly and accurately . . . because "if you weren't accurate, you were fired."

Despite the expectations of his family, Ian hardly led a distinguished financial career. He was first with Cull and Company as a trainee, and then became a partner at Rowe and Pitman's, a prominent British stockbrokerage firm.

But the young executive displayed no remarkable talent for high finance, he said later that he "was no good at it. Those financial firms are tremendous clubs, but I never could figure out what a sixty-fourth of a point was."

By 1939, he was sick of the world of finance and the City, and began to make inquiries which resulted in the Times' offer of a job as special correspondent accompanying a trade mission to Moscow.

He leapt at the chance. Although the assignment was less demanding than his coverage of the Metro-Vickers trial, he did see, first hand, the gathering storm of clouds of Europe. Hitler's final seizure of Czechoslovakia and threats to Poland pushed Fleming's reports off the front pages, and suddenly, persuading the Russians to "buy English" was not of paramount importance.

After the formal talks, the trade mission was feted socially, and Fleming again was fascinated by the security precautions of the Soviets, noting carefully, the Kremlin gate reinforced with armour plating, and the clanging alarm bells to warn of univited guests.

In March, 1939, Fleming returned to London, and war loomed imminent. About that time, his friends reported strange inquiries about his life and work, Ian Fleming was about to enter a new phase of his career — one which was instrumental in the conception of James Bond.

26

CHAPTER II

Fleming The Man

The people asking questions about Ian Fleming were from Naval Intelligence and they were recruiting. Recruiting a man with a good knowledge of languages and the City. Fleming had top-drawer recommendations from the Governor of the Bank of England, and the head of Baring Brothers, so to all appearances, he was it.

After he had been thoroughly checked out, Ian was invited to lunch at the staid Carlton Hotel by Admiral John H. Godfrey, and a couple of his anonymous minions, and asked to join the Navy as personal assistant to Godfrey, director of Naval Intelligence.

Admiral Godfrey, perhaps the father that Ian Fleming lacked, was well liked and respected by his young assistant. He was tall, broad shouldered and wore a perpetual frown, occasionally replaced by a cold grin which struck terror into the hearts of his underlings. He might well have been the model for "M", frequently described by critics as Bond's father image.

Godfrey, with Fleming's aid, soon assembled an impressive collection of men to provide the Navy with intelligence about enemy operations. The newly-recruited Intelligence operatives such unlikely types as lawyers, professors, industrial designers, reporters, geologists and geographers, were thrown into collaboration with Royal Navy Commanders and Royal Marine Majors.

Fleming operated in the precarious position of liaison man between Admiral Godfrey and his staff. Their work: cracking codes, manufacturing red herrings to draw across British trails, preparing maps, third-degreeing captured enemy spies, and training British agents for infiltration into enemy territory. It was necessary that Godfrey be advised with up to the minute efficiency of the entire operation.

Early in the War, Naval Intelligence was hard-pressed to counter the bad reputation it had received. The Royal Navy, at the time of the invasion of Norway, was plagued by inadequate knowledge of enemy movements, and the entire war effort suffered as a result. When Hitler planned to invade England, top officers of the Navy had so little faith in Godfrey's unit, that destroyers were diverted from their regular duty to bar the invaders.

Fleming, through this period, was the buffer between Godfrey and other departments of the Navy, as well as the other services. He kept a watchful eye on every member of the staff, frequently demanding early in their orientation that they provide detailed reports of their particular jurisdictions.

It must have been frustrating for Lieutenant Fleming, who already saw himself as a rather dashing figure in international intrigue, to be chained to a desk in the Admiralty office, dispatching others to perform their deeds of daring.

Fleming, at this time, was in his early thirties, and had a long, melancholy face, with clearly defined features, and clear blue eyes. He moved, as did Bond later, with grace and determination. But, apart from serving as an observer at the Dieppe raid, and on reconnaissance with the Admiral, he rarely moved from his office.

He did, however, contribute substantially to the British War effort. It was Fleming who introduced Sefton Delmer to Godfrey, as a possible agent in Lisbon. Before plans could be formulated, Delmer, along with Donald McLachlan and Robert Harling, initiated Atlantiksender, a "black" radio station, which had the destruction of German naval morale as its primary objective.

Atlantiksender, purporting at first to be run by the German Navy to provide news and entertainment for their personnel at sea and in foreign stations, broadcast in colloquial German, combining a majority of cover stories with devastating "bits of dirt."

Atlantiksender reported in great detail the raids of German cities, naming streets, which had been most heavily damaged. Even those Germans who had begun to suspect that the station was a British propaganda outlet, were impressed with the accuracy of the reporting. This accurate speculation, combined with destructive special dedications to German sailors on supposedly secret missions convinced many German naval officers, later captured, that they might as well reveal details of their operations, since the British, through some feat of black magic, already knew everything.

Black radio pulled another spectacular coup against the Italian Fleet. In September, 1943, after the invasion of Italy, Radio Livorno repeatedly warned the Italian Navy of German attempts to seize the fleet. Gradually it became obvious that Livorno was negotiating a surrender to Admiral Cunningham. And finally, on September 10, 1943, Radio Livorno ordered the Italian Navy to surrender at Malta. Probably the Italian commanding officers were aware that Livorno broadcast under orders from Cunningham, but they liked the terms of surrender, and executed its completion.

Godfrey's Naval Intelligence had earned an enviable new reputation by 1943, and even Admiral Doenitz had been brainwashed into thinking that the British knew all German secrets,.

It was in 1941, after the battle of Crete that Fleming may have received his first inspiration for Universal Export. The Germans sent an operational intelligence unit with their advance units to Crete, ordering them to seize intelligence data at British forward headquarters, evaluate it immediately, and then transmit it to Germany. Godfrey assigned Fleming to develop a British unit along the same lines.

The unit, dubbed 30AU (Number 30 Assault Unit) began to operate in the Middle East, in conjunction with the Eighth Army, and proved effective in North Africa, Sicily and Italy. Field Commanders were Quintin Riley, a former Polar explorer, and Dunstan Curtis, a lawyer. 30AU was a kind of private army, providing its members with the romance of derring do, in the absence of military discipline. During preparations for D-day in Europe, 30AU was recalled to England, so that Fleming could supervise its work.

Godfrey, by this time, had been replaced by Rear-Admiral Rushbrooke, somewhat more conservative than his predecessor.

In addition to being responsible for 30AU, and its rag-tag group of rugged individualists, Fleming was expected to oversee half a dozen other groups, scouring Europe for German intelligence information.

After his admirable performance as go-between from the special units and Admiralty officialdom, 30AU gained recognition and regard from the brass, and absorbed into the T force under General Eisenhower.

Near the end of the war, Fleming and Robert Harlach, a 30AU operative, visited Patton in Europe, and Fleming predicted that when hostilities ceased "I shall write the spy story to end all spy stories."

After the war, Fleming continued to be fascinated by intelligence and espionage operations, although he returned at last to journalism. He accepted an offer to be foreign manager of the Kemsley chain, the principal paper being the Sunday Times of London, stipulating that he receive two months vacation annually for his own writing projects.

Shortly after he started work on the Bond books, Fleming met Allen Dulles, chief of the U. S. Central Intelligence Agency and they frequently compared notes on intelligence operations. In 1962, Fleming conceded to a writer from the New York Herald Tribune that "my good friend Allen Dulles tried out two or three of the technical gimmicks in my books in CIA laboratories, and they didn't work." This meant, snorted Fleming, not that there were any flaws in the gimmicks — it was merely a strong indictment of the CIA.

Henry A. Zeiger, in The Spy Who Came In With the Gold quotes Bond's creator as telling Dulles that while the Bond books provided diversion from the cares of the day, real espionage is a deadly serious business. "It's all out war! People who raise questions about ethics, moral standards, that sort of thing, just don't understand what it's about. The head of the CIA and his opposite number in Russia, in this case Semichastney, head of Soviet State Security . . . they are absolutely like two commanders in chief in the field! . . . you see the traffic in the streets and everything's quiet and orderly here. But these two men have been locked in deadly combat for years!"

During his first few years with Kemsley chain, Fleming earned a reputation as a relentless pursuer of the whole story, and an iconoclast with a sense of humour . . . he had, said one former colleague "a highly developed sense of the ridiculous."

During the war, Fleming visited the Caribbean for the first time, and fell in love with the tropics. He made up his mind to return after the war, to build the hideaway of his dreams.

Goldeneye was built on an unused donkey racecourse near the banana port of Orcabassa. Biographer Henry Zeiger explains that the name was derived from Operation Goldeneye, a detailed plan for the defense of Gibralter, in the event a wartime attack by Spain . . . and that Fleming was probably reading Carson McCullers' Reflections in a Golden Eye, when he named the operation.

In 1946, the house where Fleming was to do most of the Bond books, was completed, and he went there each year to escape from the world and recharge his creative batteries.

Back in London, in the almost six years after the war, Ian Fleming gave every appearance of being a dedicated journalist, brimming with ideas. But still simmering in the back of his mind was that "spy story to end all spy stories." It took a surprising turn of events in March, 1952, to bring the idea to a boil.

Ian Fleming enjoyed a reputation as a habitual gay bachelor. For years, his colleagues and friends were amused and amazed by news of his successes with a parade of exotic ladies — bubble dancers, strippers, actresses and baronesses, but he scrupulously avoided lasting involvements.

Fleming was considered a good drinking companion who enjoyed interesting people and lively parties. Among his friends were writers, journalists, bankers and bureaucrats, and says Henry Zeiger "bartenders."

He had an active perpetually inquisitive mind, and was both shrewd and sensitive. Although he enjoyed deflating stuffed shirts, he was rarely cruel and never, professionally or personally played both ends against the middle.

Early in 1952, Fleming, obviously a man who enjoyed his freedom, was caught up in the chain of events which were to drastically alter his life and work.

The Daily Express, February 8, 1952, caroled: "Viscount Rothermere was granted a decree nisi in the divorce court yesterday. Lady Rothermere did not defend a charge of misconduct with Mr. Ian Lancaster Fleming, who was ordered to pay all costs."

On March 25, 1952, Ian Fleming did the British and the gentlemanly thing, he married Anne, the former Lady Rothermere. A son, Caspar, was born that same year.

After his marriage, Fleming described his ideal woman — helpful, undemanding, "I think I very much like the WREN type of woman . . . I like the fact that they seem to want to please, to make one happy . . . in the end one ends up marrying entirely the opposite of what one thinks . . . which I have done."

Ian Fleming the boy had been pushed and pulled and pummelled by a domineering, critical mother . . . Ian Fleming the man, when he finally married at the age of 43, fell victim to the vicious circle. Anne Fleming was the antithesis of the WREN type.

Robert Harlach describes her as a "slim, dark, handsome, highly strung, iconoclastic creature of middle height with a fine pair of flashpoint eyes. She has something of the air of an imperious gypsy."

Anne Fleming was one of London's most sought-after hostesses. Her "conversational" dinner parties were characterized, by good food, good wine, and highly intellectual and controversial conversation.

Immediately after their marriage, Fleming moved from his bachelor mews house in Mayfair into a large Chelsea flat overlooking the Thames. The surroundings there, according to Zieger, were not the right style for Anne Fleming, and they soon moved to a Regency, cream-stuccoed house in Victoria Square, about a hundred yards from the Buckingham Palace Riding School.

The house, with bowed windows, and built on a corner was warm and "interesting." Its overstuffed chairs and sofas, Regency furniture, Fleming's collection of black Wedgewood busts, and paintings by several Victorian artists were combined in a deceptively casual way.

The tiny dining alcove, which could seat eight comfortably was frequently crammed with a dozen or more guests, including Somerset Maugham, Evelyn Waugh, philosopher Isaiah Berlin, photographer Cecil Beaton, Malcolm Muggeridge, Noel Coward, Randolph Churchhill, poet Peter Quennel and writer Cyril Connolly.

The new Mrs. Fleming had the capacity to stimulate brilliant men . . . and parried their rapier wit with her own asp-like utterances. Ian Fleming at first, tried nobly to participate in his wife's dinner parties, and then relegated to sitting at the foot of the table with the less interesting wives, while their husbands talked with Anne at the head of the table, retreated to the Portland Club, where he played bridge for high stakes.

Geoffrey Bocca, writing in the Saturday Evening Post, June 22, 1963, referred to Anne Fleming as "a celebrated hostess, who gives some of the best parties in London." Fleming, he said, frequently succeeded in avoiding them.

Immediately before or just after his marriage in 1952, Fleming began work on the first James Bond book, Casino Royale. He said, later of his own efforts "I am not an entrant in the Shakespeare stakes. I began writing these books because my mental hands were empty, and as an antibody to my hysterical alarm at getting married at the age of 43."

Ian Fleming did not discuss the creation of James Bond with his wife. She told Canadian television interviewer Pierre Berton, with obvious resentment that the Ian Fleming who gave life to James Bond was not the man she married: "I thought," she said, "I was marrying the foreign editor of the Sunday Times," and admits that although Fleming had not mentioned his spy thrillers to her, she discovered later that he had discussed them with about five of her best friends, and three of his own.

About her husband's work, Mrs. Fleming confessed that she had never been a Bond fan . . . probably because of her distaste for the violence involved, and because Bond had no sense of humour whatever. She would have preferred, she said, that her husband had written other things — perhaps with more meaning. Biographer Ken Purdy quoted Fleming as saying that given the time, effort and concentration, he was certain that he could have written a book as meaningful as War and Peace. Anne Fleming, during her interview with Berton, expressed surprise that her late husband had said anything of the sort, and admitted that she found it difficult to believe that he could or would have written a War and Peace.

Discussing Fleming's work pattern, Anne Fleming said that her husband enormously enjoyed the research that went into the Bond books, and handled it himself. During the period when he was creating a new novel, he would work for six weeks to two months at Goldeneye in Jamaica, and then return to England where he would spend roughly six months on the rewrite.

His old friend William Plomer always read the manuscripts at that stage, and encouraged Fleming to tone down exaggerated or far fetched effects.

During the Jamaican period, he would swim early each morning negotiating a steep set of steps to reach the beach, and then return to breakfast lavishly. His three hours of morning work produced some 1500 to 2000 words, and the afternoon was devoted to rest and relaxation. Frequently he spent the evening re-reading what he had already committed to paper, and then might work for an additional hour.

Indicative of his interest in research and thorough documentation in his books, Fleming went to enormous trouble over the book jackets, supplying the gun, for instance, to the artist, and then pouring over details of the illustration. He was extremely interested in ballistics, and proud of the authenticity of his detailed work on the subject.

Despite the fact that the first publication of Casino Royale by Pan Books sold only 3000 copies, the creation of James Bond did bring Ian Fleming great financial rewards. Time Magazine, August 21, 1964, speculated that it had brought him an estimated million dollars a year from 1954-64, and paid for the London town house, spacious apartment by the sea at Sandwich, his Jamaican retreat, and luxurious offices near Fleet Street.

After taxes, Fleming had been pocketing what Time called "a few measly pence in the pound," so early in

1964, for a tax free capital gain of $280,000 he sold a 51% share of the royalties from his spy thrillers to Booker Brothers, an international investment group, headed by Sr. Jock Campbell. The author retained the other 49%.

Had Ian and Anne Fleming been willing to leave their beloved England, they could have enjoyed far more of the results of his labour. Several of their acquaintances, including author Somerset Maugham considerably reduced the government's healthy bite of their earnings, by fleeing the country. Maugham, for instance, spent his last years in France.

When James Bond as a hero was in his infancy, Anne Fleming's high brow friends were contemptuous of Fleming's efforts. One crisis in the author's marriage occured when he returned home late one evening to hear noted writer Cyril Connolly regaling the assembled guests with a dramatic reading from a Bond proof. Connolly later wrote what Anne Fleming terms a "clever parody" of Bond.

But even the highbrows are intrigued by success, and when the profits started pouring in, guests at the Fleming literary soirees became properly respectful. There was a break, however, between both the Flemings and Malcolm Muggeridge, who had professed to be an even closer friend of Ian's than of Anne's . . . and violated that friendship by writing what Mrs. Fleming called a cruel and vicious attack on her husband and his works.

Fleming, the successful author, was described in Time as tall, slimming with long graying hair. He had a passion for fast cars, gambling, golf, bridge and skindiving. Anne Fleming confirms most of those interests, but thinks that his Scottish carefulness precluded the possibility of any serious gambling on his part.

After a severe heart attack in 1961, Fleming was warned by his physicians to cut down on cigarettes, alcohol, and his more strenuous activities.

Mrs. Fleming is vehement in her condemnation of her husband's refusal to obey these edicts. He insisted, she said, on playing God with his own life, and continued to drink and smoke his usual amount, recklessly pursuing his interests in golf and under-water swimming.

By the summer of 1964, Fleming's books had sold an estimated 21 million English language copies. This included 14,500,000 U. S. paperbacks and 250 thousand American hardcovers plus another 6,500,000 hard and soft covers in England. The New York Times estimated that his books alone had brought him $2,800,000.

With the success of the three Bond movies made by 1964, all hell broke loose. The films continued to make tremendous grosses, and a double bill of Dr. No and From Russia with Love presented recently did as well second time around as it had the first. When they have completed their current run, they will have probably grossed over a hundred million dollars.

The tremendously successful films were responsible for making James Bond and Ian Fleming household words. A rash of James Bond and 007 merchandising gimmicks flooded the market, and continues to do so. Suddenly Ian Fleming himself, so often photographed and filmed on movie locations, and at post previews, was recognized wherever he went. Phyllis Jackson, his New York agent, said: "He gets an enormous kick out of being recognized. We have movie stars in the office all the time, and our secretaries never look up. But when Fleming walked in, they flocked around him."

In August, 1964, while Ian Fleming vacationed with Anne and his son Caspar at Sandwich, he suffered another heart attack. Within four hours, after reaching a hospital at Canterbury, he was dead at 56.

A gentleman to the last, Fleming apologized to the ambulance attendants who transported him "I'm sorry to have troubled you chaps" and reflected "It's all been a tremendous lark." The epitaph he penned for James

Bond in "You Only Live Twice" might have been his own: "I shall not waste my days in trying to prolong them. I shall use my time."

CHAPTER III

Ian Fleming As James Bond

Critics and fans alike have speculated whether Ian Fleming was James Bond, whether he controlled his Superhero, or the Secret Agent controlled him; and whether Fleming, in the Bond books was simply acting out his own fantasies.

Let's look at their similarities and differences, through the eyes of Fleming's wife, his fans, and the team of highly qualified psychologists, psychiatrists and psychoanalysts consulted in the preparation of this book.

Both Fleming and Bond were former naval officers. Fleming's biographer was hard-pressed to discover much detail about his career in Naval intelligence, and we never learn much about Bond's past.

Both had an uncommon (for men) interest and knowledge of scents and lotions .When Bond and Honey are led to their suite in Dr. No, the contents of the bathroom include "Floris Lime bath essence for men and Guerlain bathcubes for women. . . . the soap was Guerlain's Sapoceti Fleurs des Alpes . . . Lentheric aftershave lotion."

Tracy's hand carries the scent of Guerlain's Ode, notes Bond at an intimate moment; and Bond washes his hair with Pinaud Elixir.

Time Magazine of May 5, 1958, quotes friends of Fleming as saying that the author is "awfully like Bond . . . Floris bath essence and all."

Bond's guns, and his creator's preoccupation with researching ballistics have been the subject of much discussion. Kingsley Amis in "The James Bond Dossier" refers to a correspondence conducted between Fleming and a firearms expert named Geoffrey Boothroyd. Six years later, it was published in the Sunday Times.

It was Mr. Boothroyd, says Amis, who first dismissed Bond's beloved Beretta 25 as a ladies' gun . . . and the criticism was echoed in Dr. No, by the Secret Service Armourer, whose name, not too surprisingly was Major Boothroyd. Mr. Boothroyd, not content to criticize the Beretta, went on to say that Bond's chamois leather armpit holster would snag and foul on projecting parts of the gun, and he would be struggling to get the gun out when the other fellow is counting the holes in Bond's tummy. Mr. Boothroyd, reports Amis, made a number of constructive suggestions for Bond's armament which Mr. Fleming admits he screwed up, so that Bond sets off for Jamaica with a Walther PPK 7.65 mm *automatic* in a 'Lightning' Berns-Martin Triple Draw *revolver* holster, and with a Smith and Wesson .38 Centennial Airweight for long-range work. — Boothroyd had recommended it for close quarters and a quick draw.

At a certain stage in their development, says one Canadian psychoanalyst, almost any small boy goes through the phallic stage, where he is in love with his penis, and with his strength. It is during this phase that little boys become aggressive, with great interest in guns, and run about "shooting" everyone they meet. The gun, the analyst explains, is symbolic of the penis. Although most boys go through this phase, some never reach it, and others may be arrested in it.

Both Bond and Fleming moved gracefully and purposefully, reflecting perhaps, the physical achievement at which they both excelled. For Bond, physical achievement frequently meant the difference between destruction and survival. For Fleming, it began with the worship of his father, killed in 1917 and posthumously awarded the DSO. Then came the adulation-envy of his older brother, Peter who explored Brazilian jungles and crossed the roof of China, later recounting his adventures in widely read books. And Ian Fleming himself was an outstanding athlete during his days at Eton. He was the only boy to ever be twice named Victor Ludorum. In later life, his passion for golf and skin diving raged unabated, and he retained as his heroes Sugar Ray Robinson and Jacques Cousteau, the skin diver.

James Bond and Ian Fleming were automobile mad. Fleming gave Bond a supercharged Bentley because he liked the superhero to use "dashing" things; but also, writes Henry Zieger in The Spy Who Came In With the Gold, because he would have liked to own one himself. Fleming admitted that he had never driven a Bentley himself because he had no interest in babying cars that were highly tuned, but he did like a sporty looking vehicle, like his Thunderbird, with which, he said "he had fallen head over heels in love at first sight."

Before the Thunderbird, Fleming had owned a Standard, a Morris Oxford and then a 16-80 open Lagonda, which he gave up when he decided it would do barely 70 mph, and then changed to a souped up Graham Paige convertible, which he gave to the ambulance service at the start of World War II.

During the war, says Zeiger, Fleming owned an Opel, and after the war a Renault and a Hillman Minx, which gave way to a 2½ Litre Riley, followed by a Sapphire and a Daimler. The Daimler, Fleming said, was discarded, because of the "ugliness of the rump" . . . an interesting comment in view of the fact that Fleming frequently expounded on his theory that the buttocks, not the bosom, were the most attractive part of a woman. An acquaintance of Fleming's quarrelled with his reason for dropping the Daimler, saying that Anne Fleming had described her husband as looking like the late Queen Mary when he was behind the wheel.

After the demise of the Daimler, Fleming had reached the big money and decided to buy a luxurious car . . . he considered the Lancia Gran, then was smitten by the

Thunderbird, for which he paid three thousand pounds. According to Zeiger, Fleming claimed that his wife was indignant over the purchase, and termed the car hideous, partially because there was no room to take people to the station in it.

Fleming switched from the two seater Thunderbird to the four seater, and was a walking advertisement for American cars. After he graduated from the Thunderbird, he switched to the Studebaker Avanti, four seater, also priced about three thousand pounds.

Much has been written and said, about the symbolic passion of men for their cars. Dr. Betty Steiner, Toronto psychiatrist, calls automobile worship a classic reinforcement of masculinity. The power and speed of an automobile permits its owner to give acceptable vent to hostility, she contends, and provides reinforcement of the knowledge that he is really a man.

A Canadian psychoanalyst says that to a greater or lesser extent, many people are interested in automobiles, but that cars do frequently become symbols of masculinity and indications for narcissism. A man's automobile, says this authority, is an extension of himself, and automobile worship is closely akin to self-worship.

Bond was always impeccably dressed, black suit, string tie, short sleeved dark blue or white shirt, with loafers. Fleming exhibited many of the same tastes, and wore the clothes which were his favorites from the time of his naval discharge until his death. In London, he wore a dark-blue suit with cuffs at the sleeves, (Bond never went *that* far) a polka dot bow tie, loosely fastened, and a short sleeved blue shirt, and loafers. Wearing the same clothes daily, said Fleming, saved him from having to wonder what to wear. He hated buttons, studs and laces . . . and wore short sleeves, because he, as fastidious, as Bond, could not stand dirty cuffs.

Both Fleming and Bond were hard drinkers, and both loved dry Martinis, prepared with gentle care. Bond, however, was always particular about the manner in which his drinks were prepared, and the vintage of wines he ordered. Ian Fleming, said his wife, was happy with almost any drink, even the cheap red wine called "infuriator" which he had first consumed in his navy days.

Bond was a gourmet, with tremendous interest in food and its preparation. Fleming liked simple well-cooked food. He might have been happy subsisting entirely on scrambled eggs.

Bond, his creator frequently reminded us, was notably cruel. He came to take a good deal of pleasure in the total destruction of his adversaries, and after an illness, when "M" offered to return him to the regular service, Bond thought seriously of what it would mean to be deprived of the license to kill. Fleming, we are told, abhorred violence of all kinds. When Sir Anthony Eden visited Fleming's Jamaican retreat, and members of his party embarked on a campaign to kill bushrats which overran the estate, Fleming was upset.

But Fleming showed an unholy pleasure in questioning a former navy friend and polar explorer who had written a survival manual for escaped POW's. Delighted, Fleming questioned him about a hyopthetical situation in which a Russian stood between him and starvation. What, asked Fleming, would be the best part of a human to eat? The explorer demurred, and Fleming led him on. What about the palm of the hand? Finally, the answer came: A cut off the ribs.

As for women, both Bond and Fleming (if we are to believe the stories of his friends) enjoyed great success, and skillfully evaded involvement with a never-ending parade of gorgeous and exotic females.

Bond's attitude toward women, described for the first time in Casino Royale, was hardly flattering. ". . . women were for recreation." On a job, they got in the way and fogged things up with sex and hurt feelings, and all the emotional baggage they carried around. One had to look out for them and take care of them.

"Bitch," said Bond.

Later, in Chapter 22 of Casino Royale, Bond's thoughts of his female coworker were as follows:

"He found he could speak to her easily and he was surprised.

"With most women his manner was a mxiture of taciturnity and passion. The lengthy approaches to a seduction bored him almost as much as the subsequent mess of disentanglement. He found something grisly in the inevitability of the pattern of each affair. The conventional parabola — sentiment, the touch of the hand, the kiss, the passionate kiss, the feel of the body, the climax in the bed, then more bed, then less bed, then the boredom, the tears and the final bitterness — was to him shameful and hypocritical. Even more he shunned the mise en scene for each of these acts in the play — the meeting at a party, the restaurant, the taxi, his flat, her flat, then the week-end by the sea, then the flats again, then the furtive alibis and the final angry farewell on some doorstep in the rain."

Fleming spoke of his amorous adventures to Susan Barnes of the Sunday Express, and admitted having had an affair with a bubble dancer. The entire relationship, complained Fleming, was unsatisfactory, despite the fact that the lady was "a rather spiffing girl called Storm . . ." when the public performance was over, it was . . . " 'I'm sorry, darling, but I'm too tired. I've got to appear at the Embassy tomorrow night.' Unless you can further their careers, these actors and actresses aren't interested."

Fleming also complained, during the same interview, of American women who are sometimes too obsessed with cleanliness and bugs . . . "I had an affair with an American girl, and right after I had finished kissing her, she insisted on gargling . . . in case she'd caught something."

As for Englishwomen . . . "they're absolutely filthy.

Any hairdresser will tell you that. They think that putting on more makeup is enough."

That ruled out quite a few possibilities in "Thrilling Cities," Fleming gave short shrift to some others:

"This was my first experience of Oriental Woman, and this, and my subsequent investigations, confirmed the one great advantage she possesses for Western Man. Oriental ladies have an almost inexhaustible desire to please. They also have the capacity to make the man not only suspect, but actually believe, that he is in every respect, a far more splendid fellow than in his wildest dreams he had imagined. Not only that, but the women of the East appear, and in fact actually are, grateful for one's modest favours, with the result that every meeting with them leaves one in good humour and with a better opinion of oneself. However ill-founded this feeling may be, how very different from the knocking we all get in the West, where women — and this applies particularly to America — take such a ferocious delight in cutting the man down to size."

And Ian Fleming, if the evidence can be believed, had smarted under female domination. First his mother, later his wife, both demanding and critical . . . both with the air that Fleming didn't quite "measure up" . . . according to their standards.

Dr. Stephen Neiger, in discussing the author's background, points out that even without deprivation of father at a vital age, and without the domination of a strong mother, there is today, a great deal of confusion about the rightful male and female roles. Women demand more and more "equality," says Dr. Neiger, but don't want to pay the price which equality demands.

Fleming, himself, explained the real relationship between James Bond and his creator this way: "It's very much the Walter Mitty snydrome . . . the author's feverish dreams of what he might have been — bang, bang, kiss kiss . . . it's what you would expect of an adolescent mind which I happen to possess."

About Bond's sexual habits, Fleming said: "Perhaps Bond's blatant heterosexuality is a subconscious protest against the current fashion for sexual confusion."

Kingsley Amis, in his full-length apology for Bond, admits that Fleming's accounts of sexual relationships never seem to get much further than physical attraction ... human relations at large, he says, get a poor showing in the Bond books.

Dr. Stephen Neiger says that sexual prowess, without involvement is probably the modern man's dream.

One psychoanalyst contends that Bond, through his never-ending chain of sexual adventures is acting out phallic assertiveness. To a James Bond, he says, the sexual object is of no great importance, so long as the central character can act out "I am strong, I have a big penis, I am manly."

Perhaps, say the experts, Fleming's own experience with dominating women made him, through his hero, shy away from emotional involvement. A man in the grip of a dominating woman suffers a severe threat to his masculinity, and may be figuratively or literally rendered impotent by it.

Bond muttered that women should never have been given the vote, Fleming said his ideal woman was "helpful, undemanding and anxious to please." But Ian Fleming's mother was harsh and domineering. His wife, whom he married at 43, was sarcastic and disapproving, and socially over-shadowed her husband.

Bond was non-intellectual and rarely read, although in From Russia With Love, the agent travelling from England to the Mediterranean, he reached for his attache case, and withdrew the Mask of Dimitrios by Eric Ambler, to entertain him on his journey. True, in the next paragraph, Bond is reflecting on the remarkable and incidentally, lethal structure of the expensive looking attache case, designed for him by Q branch, rather than on the adventures of Ambler's fictional hero.

Fleming was often expected to discuss the subject of suspense fiction, and even before he was widely known as the author of the Bond books, he wrote a short summation of the New York literary scene circa 1950 for the Sunday Times, under the title "Bang-bang, Kiss-Kiss," which later became his sure fire formula for the adventures of James Bond. During discussion of the suspense novel, Fleming expressed appreciation of the masters of the American tough school, referring, say Henry Zeiger, in the Spy Who Came In With the Gold, to "the homespun American folktales of Raymond Chandler, John O'Hara, James M. Cain, 'Little Caesar' Burnett, and others who have many admirers."

Fleming's aim as an author, he said, was to write "thrillers designed to be read as literature," and cited Edgar Allan Poe, Dashiell Hammett, Raymond Chandler, Eric Ambler and Graham Greene as other practitioners of this art. James Bond he told an interviewer, was believable as a hero, and patterned after Chandler's and Hammett's heroes. He also credited his childhood favorites E. Phillips Oppenheim and Sax Rohmer with influencing his writing.

Ian Fleming was one of England's principal authorities on rare books. He began when he was first employed, to collected first editions, with the assistance of Percy Muir of Elkin-Matthews. In the days when Fleming had almost no money, Muir was a great help in locating first editions at reasonable prices. Later, after the War, Fleming became editor of The Book Collector, respected throughout the world as an authoritative publication.

Bond was an accomplished and inveterate gambler. Plots of two Bond books, Casino Royale and Moonraker, depend on desperate card contests for huge stakes. Writer Geoggrey Bocca in the Saturday Evening Post, opined that Fleming could make these scenes authoritative because he was himself a fanatical gambler. Bocca reports that, in 1941, when Fleming was travelling to Washington for secret talks, he stopped at Estoril, Portugal, with Admiral Godfrey. There, he noticed some German Intelligence agents playing chemin de fer in a Casino, and determined to relieve them of their secret funds. Unfortunately the Nazis cleaned him, and the would-be gambling shark was dependent on Admiral Godfrey for enough money to finish the journey. This experience probably led to the conception of the chemin de fer game Bond plays with the villainous Le Chiffre in Casino Royale. Not too surprisingly, Bond won that game.

After his marriage, Ian Fleming spent many evenings, when his wife was entertaining her literary friends, playing bridge for high stakes at the Portland Club.

Anne Fleming disagrees with Bocca and Zeiger about her late husband's love for gambling. He was, she observes, rather too Scotch and too careful to be very serious about it.

Bond was English, through and through. The villains he battled were always non-WASP (White Anglo Saxon Protestant). In Dr. No, for example, they reached the ultimate in non-WASPishness, and became Chigroes, or Chinese Negroes. Fleming himself, in Thrilling Cities, commented:

"India has always depressed me. I can't bear the universal dirt and squalor and the impression, false I am sure, that everyone is doing no work except living off his neighbour. And I am desolated by the outward manifestations of the two great Indian religions. Ignorant, narrow minded, bigoted? Of course *I am*."

What of this WASPism? Dr. Don McCulloch, psychiatrist at the University of Toronto, terms it nothing more or less than the acceptable British attitude. After all, he says, almost 98% of the residents of Great Britain were born there . . . England has never been a melting pot — as the United States and Canada have been, and continue to be.

Dr. Stephen Neiger, clinical pyschologist sees WASPism as manifested in Bond's adventures, as something else again. Perhaps, he says, it is considerably more insidious. Blatant prejudice and bigotry are no longer socially acceptable, when openly expressed. Perhaps the WASPism of James Bond is providing an outlet for the insecurities in all of us — it could, if it became popular enough, set back the one-world concept by a full generation.

One phychoanalyst, queried about the origins and meaning of WASPism, says that it tends to be an attempt to deny the bad, degraded, or, to a lesser extent, weak self.

And certainly, for all of us, times are changing, and people are changing. In North America, the southern states particularly, negroes want and will get, rightfully so, the right to vote, and to "move next door." Throughout the world, the working class no longer "knows its place." The working class, in fact, is fast disappearing, to give room to an increasingly large "middle class."

Ian Fleming, raised in an upper class, Edwardian English home, knew what to expect from his family and his peers, and those beneath him. His brother Peter, discussing the Soviet Union, in a book written in 1934, reprinted in 1956, said "Outside the Kremlin, where a handful of men, presumably able and partly Jewish, control (on paper) the destinies of the far-flung Soviet Republics..."

It is obvious, then, that in Fleming's family it was acceptable to point out that people are different and not worry about their reactions.

Fleming, in his writing, even falls into the old trap of believing, or pretending to believe that the non-WASP stinks. Rosa Klebb had "... the smell of the Metro on a hot evening — cheap scent concealing animal odours. People in Russia soak themselves in scent, whether they have had a bath or not . . ."

In the Spy Who Loved Me, Vivienne Michel recalls her term in an English finishing school, and her roommate, "a dusky Lebanese millionairess with huge tufts of mouse-coloured hair in her armpits . . . so dreadful, petulant, smelly and obsessed with her money" . . . obviously, in the writer's eyes, even the non-WASPs with money are repulsive.

Bond smoked more than was good for him, at least 60 custom made gold tipped cigarettes each day, and Fleming angered his wife and doctors by his persistence in doing the same thing.

Why did Ian Fleming write the adventures of Bond? Geoffrey Bocca alludes to the trick Fleming paid consistently from the moment of Bond's birth . . . leading his readers to believe that Bond is modelled on Fleming. Were Bond and Fleming one man? "Balderdash!" snorted the creator.

Writing in London's Books and Bookmen on 'How To Write A Thriller,' author Fleming said unashamedly that he did it for pleasure and money. His thrillers, "aimed somewhere between the solar plexus and upper thigh, are written for warm-blooded heterosexuals. I have no message for suffering humanity, and though I was bullied at school and lost my virginity as so many of us used to in the old days, I have never been tempted to foist these harrowing personal experiences on the public.

"I am not an angry young or even middle-aged man. I am not 'involved.' My books are not 'engaged' . . . my opuscula do not aim at changing people or making them go out and do something.

"They are not designed to find favour with the Homintern. They are written for warm-blooded heterosexuals in railway trains, airplanes or beds."

Wondering whether he might someday write the War and Peace of modern thrillers, Fleming thought it more likely that a Graham-Greene or Simeon might bring it off, because "I'm more interested in action than in cerebration . . . and I enjoy exaggeration and things larger than life. It amuses me to havé a villain with a great bulbous head, whereas, as you know, they're generally little people with nothing at all extraordinary about them."

But Anne Fleming, interviewed by Pierre Berton, disclosed that although at first, Fleming took no serious interest in Bond, having created the hero, discovered he had spawned a kind of Frankenstein's monster.

It is possible, says Dr. Don McCulloch, on the basis of the information presented, that through James Bond the superhero, the man Ian Fleming achieved his wildest dreams.

A psychoanalyst, discussing writers in general, indicates that to a greater or lesser degree, writers act out their fantasies in their work. Shakespeare, for example, was probably a reasonably well balanced man, since his works incorporated many plots and forms. Fleming, nevver too sure of himself, might have been acting out his own fantasies of phallic mastery, through the creation and adventures of James Bond.

And whether or not Fleming created Bond, his invincibility and his sexual effectiveness because of his own early father deprivation and mother domination is of little importance. The fact is that he did create a hero who could breathe life into the imaginations of millions of people throughout the world. People, says, Dr. McCulloch, who live pretty deadly lives.

CHAPTER IV

James Bond - The WASP Superhero

Fleming gave life to James Bond, and the Bond cult captured him, nurtured him . . . and lived vicariously through him. Many critics, dismissed by Bond fan Kingsley Amis as highbrows and prigs immediately questioned the name of the hero. Where, they asked wisely, did Fleming find the name Bond? Did his choice of Bond signify an abnormal interest in the subject of bondage and other dark domains?

Fleming was certainly consistent in his explanation. He was reading an authoritative text on birds of The West Indies by an ornithologist named James Bond. At the time, Ian Fleming was in search of a suitable name for his hero, whom he conceived of, says Henry Zeiger, as a blunt instrument, and wanted something flat and colorless. Immediately he saw the name James Bond, he thought — "the dullest name I've ever heard" and appropriated it.

The critics and prigs to borrow a word from Bond-fan Amis, may find the explanation unsatisfactory, and remain forever unshakeable in their opinion that there was Freudian significance in the choice of the name, but more important, for our purposes, a close look at Bond himself.

We first meet Bond in Casino Royale. It is not until Fleming is well into the plot that we learn anything of personal significance about the purposely faceless agent until he has been discovered in the casino, wearied of it, and returned to his room, where he acts out the obsessive ritual of checking for signs of intrusion. It is not until Bond retires for the night, and climbs between the harsh French sheets that we learn anything of *him*. For ten minutes, he lay, with what we will later recognize as characteristic determination, on his left side, reflecting the events of the day. Then he turned over and "focused his mind towards the tunnel of sleep." "His last action was to slip his right hand under the pillow until it rested under the butt of the .38 Colt Police Positive with the sawn barrel. Then he slept, and with the warmth and humour of his eyes extinguished, his features relapsed into a taciturn mask, ironical, brutal and cold." So we have already learned something of James Bond, the Janus-faced demi god, who does "M's" bidding.

It is not until several more pages have been turned that we learn about Bond's breakfast tastes. "After a cold shower, he sat at the writing table in front of the window. He looked out at the beautiful day, and consumed half a pint of iced orange juice, three scrambled eggs and bacon, and a double portion of coffee without sugar. He lit his first cigarette, a Balkan and Turkish mixture made for him by Morlands of Grosvenor Street, and watched the small waves lick the long seashore and the fishing-fleet from Dieppe string out towards the June heat-haze followed by a paper chase of herring gulls."

Despite Bond's early reservations about being assigned to work with a female operative, Vesper Lynd, describes him for Mathis with some interest. "He is very good-looking. He reminds me rather of Hoagy Carmichael, but there is something cold and ruthless in him."

Unhappily, Hoagy Carmichael's appearance is unknown to the younger generation. Fleming's contemporaries, said O. F. Snelling in Double 007, immediately saw the Carmichael who wrote Stardust and appeared in Hollywood films of the thirties and early forties . . . a handsome young man, indeed, Snelling suggests that Sean Connery, who plays Bond in the films, is so good that people have begun to expect Bond to be like him.

It is almost one third of the way through Casino Royale that we finally obtain Bond's description . . . the secret agent as seen by himself.

"As he tied his thin, double ended, black satin tie, he paused for a moment and examined himself levelly in the mirror. His grey-blue eyes looked calmly back with a hint of ironical inquiry and the short lock of black hair which would never stay in place slowly subsided to form a thick comma above his right eyebrow. With the thin vertical scar down his right cheek the general effect was faintly piratical."

The description had been fully developed when, in From Russia With Love, the Secret Service Agent's dossier was examined by General G of the Soviet Union's SMERSH. The photograph was described: "It was a dark, clean cut face, with a three-inch scar showing whitely down the sunburned skin of the right cheek. The eyes were wide and level under straight, rather long black brows. The hair was black, parted on the left, and carelessly brushed so that a thick black comma fell down over the right eyebrow. The longish straight nose ran down to a short upper lip which was a wide and finely drawn but cruel mouth. The line of the jaw was straight and firm. A section of dark suit, white shirt, and black knitted tie completed the picture."

Bond had graduated, we see by this description, to the knitted tie which was to become his trademark.

And then the vital statistics: "First name: JAMES. Height 183 centimetres, (described in later books as just over six feet) weight 76 kilograms; slim build; eyes: blue; hair black; scar down right cheek and on left shoulder; signs of plastic surgery on back of right hand (undoubtedly the autograph left by the SMERSH killer in Casino Royale); all-round athlete; expert pistol shot, boxer, knife thrower; does not use disguises. Languages: French and German. Smokes heavily (N. B. Special cigarettes with three gold bands); vices: drink, but not to excess, and women. Not thought to accept bribes."

". . . the man is invariably armed with a .25 Beretta atutomatic carried in a holster under his left arm. Magazine holds eight rounds. Has been known to carry a knife strapped to his left forearm; has used steel-capped shoes; knows the basic holds of judo. In general, fights with tenacity and has a high tolerance of pain."

Nearly half-way through From Russia With Love, we discover at least one reason that Bond is in such tip-top physical shape. After he awakens in the morning, and has rung the bell to indicate that he is ready to face the day, he flung the single sheet off his naked body, and swung his feet to the floor.

"There was only one way to deal with boredom — kick oneself out of it. Bond went down on his hands and did twenty slow press ups, lingering over each one so that his muscles had no rest. When his arms could stand the pain no longer, he rolled over on his back, and, with his hands at his sides, did the straight leg-lift until his stomach muscles screamed. He got to his feet, and, after touching his toes twenty times, went over to arm and chest exercises combined with deep breathing until he was dizzy. Panting with the exertion, he went into the big white-tiled bathroom and stood in the glass shower cabinet under very hot and then cold hissing water for five minutes."

After the calisthenics, Bond donned what his fans had come to recognize as his non-working uniform: "After shaving and putting on a sleeveless dark blue Sea Island cotton shirt and navy blue tropical worsted trousers, he slipped his bare feet into black leather sandals and went through the bedroom into the long-big-windowed sitting room, with the satisfaction of having sweated his boredom, at any rate for the time being, out of his body.

Bond is joined in the living room by his "jewel of a housekeeper" May, an "elderly Scotswoman with iron grey hair and a handsome closed face."

May, who is obviously devoted to Bond, maintains an

air of restrained disapproval toward him. She realizes that his work is dangerous and secret, and would die before attempting to discover any details of it.

In From Russia With Love, she maintains the habit of greeting Bond with "Good morning S . . ." Bond has teased her because she will call no man, except a king or Winston Churchill "Sir".

In Thunderball, we learn that she refers to her employer as "Mister James" and the Scotch burr has grown stronger over the years.

Despite Bond's proclivity for cutting a wide swath among the ladies he encounters, he would almost never take any of them home for his version of billing and cooing. Perhaps the admirable May is a disapproving mother figure after all.

When not working, says critic O. F. Snelling, Bond's office hours are from ten to six. Ostensibly he works for a front organization called Universal Export. This cover is used and reused by Bond in many of his adventures. "M" of course, is the head of Universal Export, as well as of Bond's division in the Secret Service.

Just when Bond is getting fed up with life at home base, he hears from "M" and is off on another exciting mission.

Bond smokes voraciously, his special Balkan and Turkish mixture, and usually (count 'em) consumes at least sixty cigarettes per day. He keeps his cigarettes in a wide gunmetal case that will hold fifty, lighting them with a battered black oxidized Ronson.

Bond, while liking the good things of life, freely admits that he is finicky, taking a ridiculous pleasure in what he eats and drinks. He explains to Vesper in Casino Royale "It comes partly from being a bachelor, but mostly from a habit of taking a lot of trouble over details. It's very pernickety and old-maidish, really, but then when I'm working I generally have to eat my meals alone and it makes them more interesting when one takes trouble."

But it's not all for nothing, the lady discovers, when she watches Bond discuss wines with the sommelier. Champagne it is Blanc de Blanc Brut 1943.

Bond's food and wine orders are likely to rate compliments from the most snooty head waiters . . . yet, in On Her Majesties Secret Service we were told that "Bond was not a gourmet.

"In England he lived on grilled soles, ceufs cocotte and cold roast beef with potato salad. It is only when travelling to far-off countries, perhaps, to help dispel the boredom of loneliness, that this meal becomes "something to look forward to, to break the tension."

Perhaps his at home consumption of roast beef has jaded his appetites a little, because Bond relies to a query in You Only Live Twice, by saying he doesn't like it.

Outside the cookbooks, says O. F. Snelling, there's been no twentieth century writer who approaches Fleming in his descriptions of delectable food.

Small wonder that after consuming all these exotic meals, Bond must go into training between Superman appearances. His two major Caribbean exploits, detailed in Live and Let Die and Dr. No, are preceded by a swimming a running course almost as taxing as the exploits themselves.

"M" the disapproving father figure to whom Bond pronounces himself "married" closes his eyes to some of Number 2's exploits and excesses, all the while advocating Spartan self-discipline and self-denial. "M" allows himself only two cheroots a day and considers any drink he wouldn't order himself as "rotgut".

Christmas, in Her Majesty's Secret Serivce falls right in the middle of a big case, and an unwilling Bond is summoned to dinner.

Instead of the drink for which he yearns, Bond is allowed a "small glass of very old Marsala, and most of a bottle of very bad Algerian wine."

Earlier, though, "M" may have been partially responsible for creating gourmet tastes in Bond. Dinner at Blades, described in Moonraker was quite an occasion. "M" started off with vodka — "pre-war Wolfschmidt from Riga," and while Bond asked for Taittinger Champagne, "M" ordered Mouton Rothschild '34 claret.

Not one to be daunted, when the vodka arrives finicky Number 2 sprinkles a pinch of black pepper on the surface to carry the fusel oil to the bottom.

The food, "M" begins with Beluga caviar, and Bond (despite his WASPishness) orders smoked salmon. "M" then has deviled kidney and bacon with peas and new potatoes, followed by strawberries in kirsch. Bond chooses lamb cutlets, the same vegetables as "M," and asparagus with Bearnaise sauce . . . with perhaps a slice of pineapple.

"M" at that stage expresses a certain admiration . . . "Thank heaven for a man who makes up his mind . . ."

Bond, his loyal readers know, always orders exactly what he wants, whether it's food, drink, or one of the endless chain of exotic females who offer themselves up to him.

Although Bond is essentially a lone wolf, and has no close friends obvious to us, he possesses an enviable natural charm, and can be companionable when he chooses to do so. The choice is always his, though, as Mathis, and Felix Leiter, and Darko Kerim and all the other co-workers discover.

But when a beautiful woman, always conforming to Bond's tastes, comes to view, Bond is off, and not running, but waiting for her to run to him at the moment *he* chooses.

Certainly all of Bond's women are passionate, when he wants them to be, and regardless of the unfortunate backgrounds which might have made them a might frigid.

And perhaps Bond-fans discover that their hero is human when they look closely at the glamourous ladies who clamor for his favors. Honeychile in Dr. No is magnificent, except for her broken nose. Domino Vitali limps just a little — because one leg is shorter than the other. Tatiana Romanov is luscious, but the muscular development (through ice skating) of her derriere leaves her a little less than perfect. And Vivienne Michel first meets Bond with her breasts exposed, or, we fear, he might not have noticed her. Pussy Galore, name or no name, is an unashamed Lesbian, and Tiffany is pathologically terrified of men.

And how does Bond acquit himself in the bedroom? "Very well" says O. F. Snelling in Double O Seven, "he loves amorous dalliance almost as much as he loves his gun, his vodka and his sea island shirts. Maybe more."

Vesper Lynd, in Casino Royale is the first conquest we are allowed to peep at. Her briefing by the Head of S warned her "don't imagine this is going to be any fun!" He thinks of nothing but the job on hand and, while it's on he's absolute hell to work for . . . He's a good looking chap, but don't fall for him. I don't think he's got much heart. Anyway, good luck and don't get hurt."

It's almost as though Vesper's superior knew she had about as much chance as the proverbial snowball in Hell, when it came to resisting Bond.

Halfway through the book, Bond relaxes a bit, and allows himself the luxury of a few nasty thoughts about Vesper. Perhaps he believes in the double standard, after all, as he "wonders about her morals. He wanted her cold and arrogant body. He wanted to see tears and essire in her remote blue eyes and to take the ropes of her black hair in his hands and bend her long body back under his."

And later, after she has been kidnapped and bundled off in an unusual and sexually arousing way "Apart from her legs, which were naked to the hips, Vesper was only a parcel. Her long black velvet skirt had been lifted over her arms and head and tied about her head with a piece of rope."

Vesper, obviously not the cool lady she had pretended to be, evidently eschewed stockings and underclothes, and only the kidnapping gave her away. Perhaps all along, she was planning to entice the ultra-desirable Mr. Bond.

As the book is racing to its dramatic close, and Bond has suffered indescribably painful, almost castrating tortures, it is Vesper, who aids so much in his recuperation. Once again, members of the Bond cult get that glimpse of Bond — unsure of himself, wondering and afraid, "that his senses and his body would not respond to her sensual beauty. Afraid that he would feel no stir of desire, and that his blood would stay cool."

But he really needn't have worried, because their affair is out of this world.

Bond, as he is to do several times during his adventures, prepares to ask the lady to marry him.

And, as he will again, he has a narrow escape when Vesper, a troubled double agent, suicides."

He recovers quickly though, as he reports to "M": "3030 was a double, working for Redland." And the book ends with Fleming's masterly touch, summarizing James Bond "Yes, dammit, I said 'was'. The bitch is dead."

CHAPTER V

The James Bond Girl

The James Bond girls, tall athletic, with straight unpolished nails and high cheekbones, move gracefully through all the adventures of the Secret Agent. Their tastes in food and drink usually echo Bond's and they use toiletries which he finds particularly appealing.

Vesper Lynd, the first James Bond girl we meet, is introduced to the invincible Bond, as his number 2, early in Casino Royale. Bond, disgruntled and apprehensive when he learns that he is to be assisted by a female operative, feels her presence strongly when they are brought face to face by liaison agent Mathis. And small wonder, for she has "very black hair," cut square and hanging low on the nape of her neck. Her eyes are widely spaced, deep blue, and they "gazed back at Bond with a touch of ironical disinterest he found he would like to shatter, roughly."

Vesper sets the pattern Bond fans will recognize as the prototype for the endless parade of Bond girls.

Lightly tanned, she wears no makeup except lipstick on a wide and sensual mouth. Her clothes exhibit just the right degree of taste and pride. The street length grey dress is enhanced by a square cut bodice lasciviously tight against her fine breasts. The skirt, finely pleated, flared from a narrow waist, is accentuated by a three-inch handstitched belt. She carries a wide cart-wheel hat in gold straw, the crown offset by a narrow black velvet ribbon. And her shoes, of plain black leather, are square toed.

Small wonder that the imperturbable Bond finds Vesper distracting and disturbing. So disturbing, in fact, that she shocks Bond's creator, the expert grammarian Ian

Fleming, into a lapse of usage when "he was quite honest to himself about the hypocrisy of his attitude towards her. *As a woman* (italics ours) he wanted to sleep with her, but only when the job had been done."

After Bond and Vesper enjoy a sumptuous dinner together, James decides (despite his obvious predatory interest in his number 2) to retreat to a safe, professional relationship. The first Bond girl is kidnapped by henchmen of the evil Le Chiffre. Bond rushes headlong into a rescue attempt and is captured himself, suffering vile, castrating tortures.

Trusty Mathis assists in their rescue from an apparently escape proof trap, and Bond undergoes recuperative care at the local hospital, with Vesper there to provide gentle reassurance. Finally the agent is pronounced well, and he and Vesper depart for an eagerly-anticipated holiday in the country. At last the sweet promise is about to be fulfilled. When the lodge proprietor leaves them talking on the threshold of Vesper's room, Bond is suddenly transported. "He pushes her inside, and closes the door, puts his hands on her shoulders and kisses her on both cheeks.

Heaven! Her eyes shine. Her hands lift to rest on his forearms. He moves against her and embraces her waist. Vesper's head goes back and her mouth opens beneath his.

"My darling," he said. He plunged his mouth down onto hers, forcing her teeth apart with his tongue and feeling her own tongue working, at first shyly then more passionately."

Bond's hands drop to her "swelling buttocks, and grip them." Vesper is panting by now, and they cling together. He seizes her hair — (he *always* grabs a Bond girl by the hair) to kiss her again. She retreats, exhausted, to the bed.

But the prize is not yet Bond's, and Vesper, with a diversionary tactic, suggests that he bathe while she unpacks, and that they get ready for dinner. Again the churning starts, and again Vesper flutters away. Bond goes swimming, perhaps instead of taking the cold shower usually recommended, and he thinks about the growing attachment between them.

Vesper had certainly crept under his skin, and over the last two weeks his feelings have changed.

There is, Bond reflects, something enigmatic and tantalizing about Vesper. She gives little of her true personality away, and no matter how long they remain together, there will always be "a private room" inside her which he can never enter.

She is thoughtful and full of consideration, without being a slavish, without compromising her arrogant spirit. And now, he has confirmed that she is "profoundly, excitingly sensual", but because of her special inner privacy, conquest of her lovely body would "always have the *sweet tang of rape*".

Enjoyment of her love would always be a thrilling voyage without the disappointment of actual arrival. She would surrender willingly, and with relish, and "greedily enjoy all the intimacies of the bend without ever allowing herself to be possessed".

When he returns to the lodge, our hero is determined to claim his prize. They dine lavishly on the terrace. Vesper pleads weariness, and returns to her room shortly after nine.

At nine-thirty, Bond steps through the adjoining bathroom, into her room. Romantically, the "moonlight shone through the half-closed shutters and lapped at the secret shadows in the snow of her body on the broad bed".

The next morning at dawn, Double O Seven woke in his own room, and went quietly out to swim. He has determined that "that day he would ask Vesper to marry him. He is quite certain. It was only a question of choosing the right moment."

The swashbuckling romantic hero is about to step, with eyes wide open, into a snare of his own making. Or is he?

Bond re-enters the hotel, and is surprised to see Vesper emerging from the telephone booth. She is startled by his arrival, and contrives a lame explanation about enlisting Mathis' aid in obtaining a frock.

Gallant Bond does not question her further, to her obvious relief, but returns to his room.

The episode is shattering and "the end of the integrity of their love. The succeeding days were shambles of falseness and hypocrisy mingled with her tears an moments of animal passion to which she abandoned herself with a greed made indecent by the hollowness of their days."

Bond tries several times to break down the mutual mistrust and insecurity but he is unsuccessful. Vesper shows real terror when a man wearing a sinister black eyepatch arrives in a black Peugeot saloon.

Their next few days are much the same. The man in the Peugeot is back again, and Vesper's face is cold as stone. Bond makes one final attempt to break down the barrier. He begs her to tell him what's wrong, and confesses that on that first morning, he was returning to propose. He pleads for a new start. "What is this dreadful nightmare that is killing us?"

"You mean you would have married me? . . . My God, My God."

A new numb note of resignation comes into her voice, and Vesper squares her shoulders, promising to tell Bond everything the next morning.

That night, "for two hours they made a slow sweet love in a mood of happy passion which . . . Bond would never have thought they could regain."

Vesper weeps anew as she looks intently at Bond, and bids him goodnight.

The next morning, Bond is wakened by the patron,

and he rushes to Vesper's room to discover her — dead.

He opens the letter she had left, reading quickly after the first few words, and then throwing it onto the bed.

"Goodbye, my darling" wrote the beautiful, troubled Bond girl, "I am an agent of the MWD. . . . a double agent for the Russians."

The explanation which follows is logical and might ordinarily inspire sympathy. Lovely, cool Vesper had been trapped into the double dealing role, under pressure impossible to withstand.

Bond wiped his fingers together as though they had been soiled by the letter. He struck his fist against his temple, and stood up, looking out over the sea. "Then he cursed aloud, one harsh obscenity."

"His eyes were wet and he dried them."

As he prepares to place a call to London, Bond reviews the facts quite calmly. He sees Vesper now as just a spy. "Their love and his grief were relegated to the boxroom of his mind. "Later, he may haul them out, scrutinize them clinically, then resentfully thrust them back with "other sentimental baggage he would rather forget."

Bond, now the dedicated super agent can think only of Vesper's betrayal of him, the Service and Britain. He speculates on the damage it had done.

Bond reflects on his game of "Red Indians" through the years while Vesper figuratively walked down a corridor with vital documents in her hand. On a tray . . .

The London call comes through, and Bond is talking to the outside Liaison officer in London, the only one he is permitted to telephone from abroad .. . in case of dire necessity.

". . . 007 speaking . . . emergency . . . pass this on . . . 3030 was a double, working for Redland . . . bitch is dead now."

So, the tough, single minded Commander Bond allowed himself to get involved, for a few days, and is now undergoing self-flagellation for his weakness. His rage is murderous.

But, of necessity, Secret Agents who live with danger are resilient . . . and the sexual drive is like the hunger or thirst for food or drink — it must be appeased, as painlessly as possible — in a new Bond book.

Solitaire is the next Bond-Girl author Fleming's hero meets, and this time, the lady is one of the most beautiful women Double O Seven had ever seen. He meets Solitaire — the first of what O. F. Snelling calls "the female weirdies who march regularly through the Bond books" in Live and Let Die.

Solitaire's real name is Simone Latrelle. She is pale, with blue eyes, luxuriant short blue black hair, nails unpainted, and again the wide sensual mouth which appeals to Bond and his readers. Solitaire appears to be a captive virgin princess under the protection of Mr. Big, a fiendish Negro gangster huge in proportion who doubles as a SMERSH agent.

Mr. Big, with uncharacteristic gallantry, plans to marry the girl. Solitaire, who was born in Haiti has an aptitude for telepathy. It will be interesting, he muses to see their children . . . but that joy will have to be postponed, because "for the time being she is being difficult. She will have nothing to do with men."

That, was before she met Bond . . . and what a difference the meeting makes. Within seconds of Solitaire's introduction to Bond, Mr. Big's prisoner, at the time, she engages in an old-fashioned game of kneesies with him, and "nonchalantly draws her forearms together in her lap so that the valley between her breasts deepens." A lot of the Bond girls, as any member of the Cult will tell you, use this same device regularly.

Solitaire has been assigned by Mr. Big to read the agent's mind, and establish the truth of what he says. But she appears to be on Bond's side from the beginning. Bonds charms can hardly be blamed for her warmth however, because he is strapped to a chair, with a concealed gun trained on him and Mr. Big is watching every flicker.

The eagle-eyed villain notices Bond's slight response to Solitaire's come-on, and smartly lashes the girl across the shoulders.

That was a mistake, obviously, because she becomes completely sympathetic to Bond, and inclined to bite the hand of Mr. Big who has been protecting and nurturing her since he picked her out of the proverbial gutter.

Naturally, Bond escapes and helps Solitaire make a run for it. Embarking by train from New York's Penn Station they head south for St. Petersburg, Florida.

Conditions for billing and cooing seem just right, with Bond and Solitaire forced to represent themselves as a married couple, cooped up in a Pullman compartment.

But Bond is still on the job. Mr. Big's spies have eyes everywhere, and it's important for Double 0 7 to keep his wits. However, he can't turn his back on an attractive woman, especially such an aggressive one, so, despite a broken finger, (souvenir of the visit with Mr. Big), Bond holds her in his good arm, and kisses her.

"She took his face between her two hands and held it away, panting. Her eyes were bright and hot. Then she brought his lips against hers again and kissed him long and lasciviously, as if she was the man and he the woman." Poor Bond and poor Fleming . . . doomed to spend their lives surrounded by aggressive women bent on reversing the roles of the sexes.

This sexually awakened nymph is really turned on. But Bond's good sense prevails, and he insists that they get some sleep. A gentleman, no matter what the provocation, and Solitaire is certainly provocative. Bond retires to the room next door, so that Solitaire may undress for bed. He returns to a compartment heavy with the scent of Balmain's Vent Vert, to find celestial Solitaire in the upper bunk, propped up with the bedclothes pulled high. Underneath, she's mother naked, and Bond finds her revelation of this fact tantalizing. Exercising his usual restraint, he reaches up, to plant a goodnight kiss on her cheek, but she reaches for him. Says the seductive lady: "It's fun for me to be able to tease such a strong silent man. You burn with such an angry flame. It is the only game I have to play with you and I shan't be able to play it for long." She drops back to sleep, entreating Bond to get well quickly.

Their adventures permit little time for lovemaking, and too soon they are recaptured by Mr. Big who has conceived a suitably diabolical punishment for them. Bond and Solitaire, prisoners on a ship in Jamaican waters are sentenced to be tied together and dragged through shark-infested water to provide tasty snacks for the creatures. Solitaire is stripped naked, and she and Bond are finally face to face — not quite the way they would have planned it.

They suffer many dreadful wounds in the course of this sport but are saved from drowning by a coral reef, which Mr. Big had intended should flay them. As a fleet of canoes skims out to rescue them, "the first tears since his childhood" well up in Bond's eyes and run down into the bloodstained sea.

But what of last year, when he shed a token tear or two for Vesper Lynd . . . the bitch who is now dead?

As a reward for a job well done, "M" cables Bond permission for a fortnight's "passionate leave". Can the old curmudgeon really mean that, or is it a typographical error?

At this point in Bond's second adventure, members of the Cult are not surprised to find that several raw and bleeding wounds prevent him from taking immediate advantage of Solitaire's sexy promise. A brazen barracuda has taken a large bite out of his shoulder, and he is raw and bleeding in a hundred places. Solitaire, too, is pretty badly marred, but as luck (and 007) would have it there'll be no permanent disfigurement of the lovely creature, and that "passionate leave", promises to be extremely useful.

We get halfway through the next Bond book, Moonraker, before the Bond-girl puts in an appearance. Bond, between assignments, is summoned by the crusty "M" to do him a personal favor, of a delicate nature.

"M", is a member of Blade's, a St. James area gambling club, in the grand old British tradition. Deucedly awkward though it may be, he suspects Sir Hugo Drax, a millionaire member, of cheating at cards. The situation is doubly appalling because Sir Hugo is internationally renowned as the man who is personally financing the launching of a British guided missile called Moonraker.

Bond discreetly manages to discover that Sir Hugo *h*as been playing fast and loose with the rules. With the aid of a highly polished cigarette case which enables him to see other hands the gentleman has made several coups. Bond, true to form, unmasks the rascal, in a four-handed fight to the death.

Drax of course, does not exactly relish his public humiliation, discreet though it may have been, and determines to get even with Bond if the opportunity arises. It does, when a German scientist on the Drax Moonraker site shoots and kills an Air Ministry Security officer. Bond gets the assignment.

The German claimed as his motivation that the officer he shot had cut him out in his romantic bid for a lady with the improbable name of Gala Brand. Miss Brand, incidentally, is a policewoman, doing undercover work for the Special Branch, who has infiltrated the project as Sir Hugo's private secretary. She has gained a lot of technical knowledge about the rocket project, but has never reported anything amiss.

Bond takes the usual cram briefing prerequisite on all dangerous assignments. He starts out for the rocket base, thinking: The girl? He would have to be careful how he contacted her and careful not to upset her. He wondered if she would be of any use to him. After a year on the site she would have had all the opportunities of a private secretary to the Chief to get under the skin of the whole project — and of Drax. And she had a mind trained to his own particular craft. But he would have to be prepared for her to be suspicious of the new broom and perhaps resentful. He wondered what she was really like. The photograph on her record-sheet at the Yard had shown an attractive but rather severe girl. Any hint of seductiveness had been abstracted by the cheerless jacket of her policewoman's uniform.

Hair: Auburn. Eyes: Blue. Height: 5 ft., 7. Weight: 9 stone. Hips: 38. Waist: 26. Bust: 38. Distinguishing marks: Mole on upper curvature of right breast."

"Hmm," mused Bond.

When our hero did meet the Gala lady face to face, he was not at all disconcerted by her apparent lack of interest in him, and what may have been a touch of hostility toward him. "It crossed Bond's mind that she had been well-chosen. Reserved, efficient, loyal, virginal. Thank heavens, he thought, a professional."

During the dinner which followed his arrival, James Bond was seated between Sir Hugo and Miss Brand. She answered his attempts at polite conversation in monosyllables, and avoided his glance. Bond, ever the super lover, became annoyed at her lack of response.

Certainly, Bond found Gala Brand far more attractive than the austere photograph had promised. There was authority in the definite profile, but it was relieved by sooty lashes sweeping over dark blue eyes. The side mouth, he observed, might have been painted by Marie Laurencin, save that the lips were too full, and the glossy back hair curving in at the base of the neck was arranged differently.

The severe dinner dress, in charcoal black grosgrain was relieved by full sleeves just below elbow length, and the wrap-over bodice revealed the swell of the splendid breasts Bond had anticipated after glancing at her record sheet. At the point of the vee, reposed a blue cameo brooch, and on her engagement finger, a half hoop of small diamonds.

In the fashion that members of the cult have come to expect from Bond-girls, Gala wore no makeup other than a warmly hued lipstick, and the no-nonsense finger nails were square cut, and polished in a natural shade.

Double O Seven, in his usual manner, reducing every attractive woman to the common denominator of a personal sex object, concluded that she was lovely, and beneath that British reserve, very passionate. Gala might be a commendable officer and a jujitsu expert, but Bond knew about that mole on her right breast.

Gala Brand, meanwhile has several thoughts about the dashing secret service man, who has been imposed on her. Why, she wondered, couldn't the assignment have been given to one of her friends from the Special Branch? And just how would the romantic, good-looking secret service man, with the cruel mouth and cold eyes, occupy himself with no beautiful spies to make love to. She determined to be friendly — on her own terms with the agent, who might have been dreamed up, she thought by Phillips Oppenheim.

At their next meeting, in the presence of Drax, Bond develops an admiration for the professional half of Gala, and after seeing more of her, retains his curiosity about Gala the woman. Sir Hugo suggests that Bond spend part of the afternoon inspecting the beach and bottom of the cliff on the rocket site, and that because "two pairs of eyes" . . . were better, he should take the frosty Miss Brand with him.

The beautiful green and blue and gold May afternoon creates the setting, and Gala appears in exotically gay clothes . . . a black and white striped cotton shirt, tucked into a wide hand stitched black leather belt, above a medium length skirt in shocking pink . . . Bond barely recognizes her as the chill woman of the previous evening.

They do devote some time to business, though, before Bond prevails on Gala to swim with him, attired in the "bits and pieces" she must be wearing underneath. Blushing a little in a suitable manner, she thinks of her almost transparent bra and panties. Gala is typical however and lets herself be persuaded. She goes behind a rock to undress.

The irrepressible Bond dives underwater, and surfaces beside Gala. "She felt the quick tight clasp of his arms around her and the swift hard impact of his lips on hers."

Gala damned him but her tingling awareness of the golden afternoon ensured her quick forgiveness, and, soon she was lying beside him on the beach, ostensibly waiting for their impromptu swimming costumes to dry out, and gazing up at the blue sky, and the chalk white cliff.

With the "beautiful strapping body of the girl," . . . incredibly erotic in the tight emphasis of the clinging brassiere and pants" beside him, Bond begins to shrewdly calculate the extra time at his disposal. The fifteen minutes to spare before they would have to start back should be. . .

He broke his "hot crouching thoughts" and returned to small talk. Then, boom! The cliff above them is

dynamited and Bond throws himself on top of Gala
. . . his face pressed into her cheek, aware that the air is full of thunder, and that they are being buried in rocks and chalk dust.

Their nearness to the cliff had spared them, and Bond clawed out, inch by inch, with torn and bloody hands. The few clothes they had been wearing were torn off, and blood from Bond's badly cut back and arms dripped down and mingled with the chalk dust. Finally, they reach clear beach, lie exhausted for awhile, and then, naked and unashamed, enter the shallows to get rid of the choking dust which covers their bodies.

Fortunately for the proprieties their outer garments lay safely on the rocks, a few yards away from the cliff fall. They dress, engage in a touch of intimacy when they share Gala's comb, and relax with cigarettes.

After cleaning up and dining nearby, they taxi back to Sir Hugo's house. The company seems startled to see them arrive.

There's little time for romance now. Gala discovers that Drax really plans to destroy London with the rocket, and Bond, suspecting the same thing is hot in pursuit.

Gala, always versatile, gets caught picking Sir Hugo's pocket, and Drax and cohort truss her up and cart her off to captivity.

Later the enemy contrive to force Bond's car — this time a Bentley, to crash while in pursuit and they imprison the unconscious agent.

Confined with the girl and trussed in bonds of biting copper wire, Bond gets an inspiration, and proves that he is truly invincible, as he ignites a desk lighter with the use of his teeth and uses it to ignite a blow torch, burning through the wire binding Gala. In seconds, she has freed him, and gives him a grateful kiss, as no Bond girl would fail to do.

Later, trapped in an elevator shaft, the nasty, resourceful villains turn a steam hose on them. Poor Bond . . . in this romance, he is fated to employ the ageless positions of love again for protection as he wraps himself around Gala to shield her. Inevitably, the evil Drax is foiled, and Bond permits himself to conject an interlude with Gala *after* she has been received at the palace. But his hopes are dashed when she informs him that she has a previous engagement, to Detective Inspector Vivian, whom she will marry the following day.

Once again . . . Bond the romantic superhero has escaped involvement, this time in spite of himself.

Bond's next assignment is rather more like it, as he is detailed to break up a diamond-smuggling gang. Fortunately he looks a lot like the fellow employed to do the carrying, and can deceive his gang contact, appropriately named Tiffany Case.

When he reports for duty, there is Miss Case, described as a 27 year old single American, reportedly quiet of habit. She is sitting half-naked, astride a chair in front of the dressing-table, gazing across the back of the chair into a mirror. Her bare arms are folded along the tall back of the chair and her chin is resting on her arms. Her spine well arched, there is arrogance in the set of her head and shoulders. The black string of her brassiere across the naked back, the tight black lace pants and the play of her legs whip at Bond's senses.

The vital statistics are what we have come to look for in the Bond girls . . . 5 ft. 6, heavy long blonde hair, and eyes which change from light gray to deep grey-blue. Lightly tanned skin, without adornment except the deep red lipstick.

She is unconcerned with the informality of her attire, and remains in the room listening to a record which had "her brazen sexiness, the rough tang of her manner . . . and poignancy that had been in her eyes as they had looked moodily back at him out of the mirror."

When Tiffany does get around to dressing for the street, she displays the traditional good taste we expect of the Bond-girl . . . a smart black tailored suit, over a deep green olive shirt, golden tan nylons, and square toed black crocodile shoes. Her tasteful jewelery . . . a slim gold wristwatch, with black strap, and a heavy gold chain bracelet. And because, diamonds are her business, a large baguette cut diamond on her right hand. Her soft, sullen lips gave the effect of a "sinful" mouth. . . Not, thought Bond, judging by the level eyes, the authority and the tension behind them, one that often . . . or recently had sinned.

Tiffany doesn't immediately fall panting into the agent's arms, but she doesn't give him the Gala freeze either. She is matter-of-fact in discussing his assignment, cheerful but a trifle hard boiled. Her dryly delivered instructions mark her as a capable businesswoman, even if the business if a trifle illegal.

Tiffany's eyes are evidently more articulate than most, because during their short initial interview, they transmit a no-nonsense message to Bond. "Sure. Come and try. But, Brother, you'd better be tops."

Her cool business-like approach is shaken a bit when he suggests a Friday night date in New York. After stammering and looking away, Tiffany agrees to an eight o'clock meeting at "21."

In New York, after delivering the contraband diamonds, Bond encounters his old friend Felix Leiter, now a Pinkerton's man, and hears Tiffany's life history. From childhood, she's been on the fringe of the gangs. Her mother ran "the snazziest cat house" in San Francisco, and was successful until she defied the local gang's demand for protection money. One night the mob turned up, wrecked the place, and ignoring the girls, subjected Tiffany, 16, to a gang bang. The next day, she lifted her mother's cash box . . . and struck out on her own. After working as a hat check girl, taxi dancer, studio extra and waitress, at about twenty, she started serious drinking. She rescued a child from drowning, and came to the attention of a rich woman who hired her as companion, introduced her to Alcoholics Anonymous, and took her around the world. When they returned to San Francisco, Tiffany went back to her mother for awhile and ended up shortly afterwards in Reno. As a result of her brutal sexual initiation she won't have anything to do with men . . . and her stand-offishness impressed Seraffimo Spang, a minor villain so much that he hired her to work at the Tiara Club in Las Vegas. For the last few years, she has remained there, between her excursions to Europe.

Still on her first drink Tiffany warns Bond "I'm not going to sleep with you . . . don't waste your money getting me tight." She relents a little though, and shifts to feminine flirtatiousness, when she asks him to say something nice about her dress.

Bond tells her it's a dream. He loves black velvet, he says, especially against a sunburned skin, and he's glad she doesn't wear too much jewelry or paint her fingernails. Gallantly, he terms her the prettiest smuggler in New York.

Bond has said the right thing. Tiffany drinks slowly, accepts a cigarette and leans forward for a light. In the Bond girl tradition, "the valley between her breasts opened for him." Those articulate eyes are busy again, and they signal "I like you . . . all is possible between us . . . don't be impatient . . . please be kind, I don't want to be hurt any more."

They eat well and drink well, and Tiffany, a little sozzled by this time, suggests that Bond take her back. He discovers then, that she too is staying at the Astor. They travel with the silence of a married couple who've had a row, and end the evening in silence. Bond gets off the elevator at her floor and walks with her to her room. She whirls angrily on him so that he sees the tears in her eyes. Then Tiffany embraces him fiercely, and tells him to look after himself, "I don't want to lose you." She pulled his face against hers, and kissed him hard and long but tenderly, almost sexually. As soon as Bond puts his arms around her, she must escape, the sultry glow back in her eyes. She slams and locks her door . . . and that's that. As a Bond buff would expect, however, the war has not yet been lost.

Bond's duty takes him to Las Vegas, where he finds Tiffany working as a card-sharping dealer in Seramo's casino. He disobeys a no-gambling edict imposed by one of his diamond-smuggling employers, and is grabbed by Seraffino's tough boys. Not just for disobeying the rules, but because by now members of the gang suspect that he is cop or private eye. After he has been delicately worked over by a couple of dancers in football spikes, and is in the inevitable bruised and bleeding condition, Tiffany helps him escape, and they are on their way to New York.

She has obviously warmed to him and Bond "knew that he was very near to being in love with her." If the romance ripens, Bond realizes that it may become permanent. "Once he had taken her by the hand it would be forever. . . . He would . . . be the healer, the analyst to whom the patient had transferred her love and trust on the way out of her illness."

On their way across the Atlantic aboard the Queen Elizabeth, the relationship has deepened. Before long, Tiffany is asking what kind of girl would suit him.

Always the charmer, Bond describes Tiffany, explaining that his dream woman must be able to make Sauce Bernaise as well as love.

"Would you marry her?" asks Tiffany.

"Not necessarily," replies Bond. "I'm almost married

already. To a man. Name begins with M. I'd have to divorce him before I tried marrying a woman. And I'm not sure I'd want that."

Tiffany *is* a remarkable girl and a true example of the Bond-girl type. This bit of intelligence doesn't send her fleeing for the hills.

Tiffany's libido gets the Bond message, and as he is taking her to her cabin, Bond finds himself being pulled toward his own cabin. "I want it to be in your house, James."

There, the Tiffany Bond suspected and the fans always knew had to be, shows her self. "And after a while his other hand (one had seized her hair, of course) went to the zip fastener at the back of her dress, and without moving away from him she stepped out of her dress and panted between their kisses, "I want it all, James. Everything you've ever done to a girl. Now. Quickly."

Bond bent down and put an arm round her thighs and picked her up and laid her gently on the floor.

Obviously the newly uninhibited Tiffany deserved something other than that comfortable Queen Elizabeth bed.

After another brush with the gang, Bond rescues Tiffany this time, and thinks ahead to "an age of sleep with her dear body dovetailed against his and his arms around her forever."

No sooner the thought than the antidote. This time the eyes talking to Bond are those of a dead gangster, saying: "Mister. Nothing is forever. Only death is permanent. Nothing is forever except what you did to me."

And, then there was Tatiana, Corporal Tatiana Romanova, to be specific. Of the Soviet MGB. Tatiana doesn't actually meet Bond until almost half way through "From Russia With Love," but all the Bond fans knew she would. Because: "One of her early boy friends had said that she looked like the young Greta

Garbo. . . . Fine dark brown silken hair brushed straight back from a tall brow and falling heavily down almost to the shoulders, there to curl slightly up at the ends, a good, soft, pale skin with an ivory sheen at the cheekbones; wide apart, level eyes of the deepest blue under straight natural brows, . . . long lashes, . . . a straight rather imperious nose."

And the mouth — it probably looked terribly wide when she smiled . . . full lips, delicately drawn. Tall, (she had abandoned her training in the Leningrad ballet school when she grew an inch over the 5' 6 limit), faultless arms and breasts, and a derierre just a bit too well muscled, from the figure skating ability which had placed her on the first Dynamo women's team.

Tatiana, dedicated, uncomplicated and as beautiful as the assignment demands was chosen by SMERSH to lure and destroy the dangerous and troublesome James Bond. With a story of how she fell in love with his photograph, and admired the SMERSH file of his exploits, she manages to convince the contact she wants to defect to the West. If he will assist her in this, she will deliver a new cipher machine as part of the bargain. Bond, though, must travel to Istanbul to pick up the combination package.

Tatiana, the magnificent, unquestioningly loyal Soviet soldier has accepted the peremptory orders of her superiors, instructing her to give her maidenly all for the attraction and seduction of the offensive Mr. Bond. Darko Kerim, Britain's undercover Turkish agent, has been chosen to pass the word of her infatuation to Bond and the Secret Service.

Neither "M" nor Bond are idiots, but they haven't yet discovered what the catch is. And Tatiana, lovely child, has swallowed the sugar coated Soviet story that Bond must be discredited . . . she knows nothing of the hired assassin who will finish the job she starts.

The resourceful Darko Kerim arranges Bond's first

glimpse of Tatiana, through a periscope concealed under Societ headquarters in Istanbul.

He sits recalling that moment, thinking of the tall beautiful girl with the "dancer's long gait" who walked into the Soviet conference room carrying a document. She crossed to her chief, and every man at the conference table looked up. The expressions on their faces had been strange. More than admiring. More than lecherous. They were curious. But there was also, Bond thinks, contempt? For what? Why? They looked at her with the eyes of "respectable" people staring at prostitutes. Did they already suspect her planned defection?

Later, Bond is relaxing after what started as an evening out with Kerim, and ended with a somewhat exhausting brush with a few minor villains. He has just showered, and finally stands naked, admiring the view from his darkened window. Just as he bends to switch off the last lamp, a sound makes him stiffen.

A nervous giggle came from the shadows at the back of the room, and the unnerved hero heard a girl's voice: "Poor Mister Bond. You must be tired. Come to bed."

Too much of the grape? Punch drunk? Dreaming? Bond whirled to the bed, and turned on the lamp. "There was a long body under the single sheet. Brown hair was spread on the pillow. The tips of the fingers showed, holding the sheet up over the face. Lower down the breasts stood up like hills under snow."

Bond laughed, and reached — to give the hair a soft tug. He sat on the edge of the bed, and waited until one corner of the sheet was lowered, and one enormous blue eye "inspected him."

"You look very improper," said the muffled voice, noting his nakedness.

Bond then sets out to discover how his late date reached his room and his bed. After he threatens to get into bed, she blushingly pulls herself up on the pillows with a traditional "Oh no, you mustn't."

Tatiana seems to be a most uncommunal tease. Because nudity is not what the young lady considers "kulturny" . . . for him at least, Bond dons one of the dark blue silk pajama coats he affects, and sits down to tell Tatiana that "You are one of the most beautiful women in the world."

After he has heard that Tatiana considers him very handsome . . . like an American film star, Bond is properly insulted, and immediately begins to negotiate his visitor's defection to the West . . . with cipher machine. Tatiana, innocent that she is, obviously believes that she must seduce Bond for the sole purpose of a "harmless konspiratsia." They discuss traveling by train to London, and Tatiana longs for those four days with him "in the little house on wheels . . . it had been her duty to force him. Now it was her passionate desire."

And what else — she *is* a Bond girl.

Bond moves closer, takes her hand, and gazes into the eyes of his unlikely Russian soldier. He sees only happiness there, and that she wants him to love her, and is surprised at what is happening. Suddenly "Tatania's other hand came up and round his neck, and pulled him fiercely down to her." At first the mouth trembled under his, and then, as passion took her, the mouth yielded into a kiss without end."

That does it . . . the love game is on. But above them, behind a gold framed mirror over the bed of the honeymoon suite two photographers from SMERSH sit close together in a tiny cabinet 'de voyeur'.

"The view finders gazed coldly down on the passionate arabesques the two bodies formed and broke and formed again, and the clockwork mechanism of the cine cameras whirred softly on and on as the breath rasped out of the open mouths of the two men and the sweat of excitement trickeld down their bulging faces into their cheap collars."

That train journey of theirs is an eventful one. There are games of "kneesies" and there are interruptions from friend Darko, who wants to warn Bond that Tatiana is likely going to pull a double cross. But Bond trusts her. There'll be no lovemaking, or sleep for that matter, until the dangers are past. He is protective, though, and Tatiana slumbers peacefully in his arms. Eventually Bond rests, with his head cradled on Tatiana's lovely lap. As though she had been waiting for the opportunity, she takes his face in her hands, gazes deeply into his eyes, and asks urgently, "Dushka, how long shall we have this? . . . For long, replies Bond . . . But how long, she demands?

With Bond, not for very long. Lovely though the lady is, she is an enemy agent. Her future . . . a new name, a new identity and life in Canada (The British Secret Service seems to ship awkward defectors to the Canadian hinterland) and an annuity, perhaps a thousand pounds a year.

Bond copes with the SMERSH assassin who has been meant, all along, to exterminate him . . . ignominiously, and revives Tatiana, who has been drugged to prevent her interference with the planned assassination.

There's no walk into the sunset for Bond and the comely Communist. This time the Bond girl doesn't even get the benefit of violent elimination from the life of Double O Seven. Even the members of the Bond cult just wait and wonder.

Bond usually finds the Bond girls gift wrapped to please, but Honeychile Rider, at first glimpse in Dr. No, is unwrapped. Our hero is skulking on the beach of a guano island near Jamaica, checking the nefarious activities of another unWASP villain, Dr. No, when his attention is caught by a moving shadow. Again, he stiffened, and again the Bond heart missed a beat . . . "his eyes, as he stared through the blades of grass, were fierce slits."

The sight which provoked such strong reactions? A not quite naked beauty. She wore the usual broad leather belt around her waist . . . and no clothes at all. The belt, with a hunting knife reposing in the leather sheath at her right hip, made her nudity "extraordinarily erotic."

She stood in the "classical relaxed pose of the nude, all the weight on the right leg and the left knee bent . . . the head to one side as she examined the things in her hand.

It was, Bond observed, a beautiful back, a pale all-over cafe au lait effect, with "the sheen of dull satin. The gentle curve of the backbone was deeply indented, suggesting more poerwful muscles than usual . . . the behind firm and rounded as a boy's. The legs were straight and beautiful, and no pinkness showed under the slightly lifted left heel. She was not a coloured girl." Fortunately for Bond, we must suppose.

The ash blonde hair, hung to shoulder length and framed the side of her cheek in set strands. A green diving mask was pushed above her forehead, and the green rubber thong bound her hair at the back.

Why is she there? Not for him. Not now at least, the girl is hunting sea sheels and whistling Marianne. As she pauses to stretch and yawn, Bond joins the chorus and startles her. Slowly the realization that there is actually someone else there dawns, and her hands fly to cover her . . . one to the loins, the other to the face, covering below her eyes, which are wide with fear. Bond identifies himself as another trespasser, and hopes she won't be frightened. The hand drops from her face, closes around the knife. Bond looks more carefully at the face and understands why the lovely nymph rushed to cover it.

She is beautiful, with wide apart deep blue eyes under sun bleached lashes. The mouth is wide and full. The face is serious, the jawline determined, an independent face. Once, perhaps only once, the barefoot nymph had failed in her independence. For the "nose was badly broken, smashed crooked like a boxer's." Bond stiffened, this time with revolt at what had befallen the supremely beautiful girl.

They talk, guardedly, and Bond discovers that the wild little creature comes often to the island . . . despite the owner's active aversion to trespassing and trespassers. She knows that it is a dangerous place, and enjoys it.

The two trespassers exchange names and when Bond, courtly even in these surroundings and circumstances, says that he is glad to meet her, Honey suddenly becomes aware of her nakedness. She announces that she must get dressed, begins to stoop to pick up her shells, and then realizes that she will be exposed and vulnerable if she does. After warning Bond sharply not to touch her seashells, Honey walks stiffly to disappear behind some rocks.

Bond waits and wonders. He has already almost forgotten her deformity. The broken nose had "somehow slipped away behind his memory of her eyes and her mouth and her amazingly beautiful body." He found her imperious attitude and "quality of attack exciting."

Bond turns to greet her as she returns clad in rags, a faded brown shirt and knee length patched cotton skirt, fastened with the leather belt. She carried a canvas knapsack over one shoulder.

Bond and Honey discuss the island, the villainous "Chinaman" and his fire breathing dragon, a creature the agent can't accept just yet.

The two, and Bond's sidekick, a Cayman Islander named Quarrell are thrown together for mutual protection, when No's gunmen and fire breathing dragon

— actually a converted lorry — start tracking them.

Bond and his nature girl exchange life histories, and he discovers that her father and mother died in a fire which destroyed their house when she was five. Her parents, from one of the old Jamaican families, left no money, and Honey was brought up by her devoted black nanny, with whom she lived in the cellar of the burned out house. The nanny, unfortunately, died when Honey was just 15, leaving the girl with a pile of old books left over from the fire. Said Honey proudly, "I started with A when I was about eight. I've got as far as the middle to T."

Honey loves animals, and mistrusts humans . . . understandable enough, when she explains to Bond that, after her nanny died, a local white overseer began urging her to move to his house. He invaded her cellar one night and "fought with me because I wouldn't do what he wanted me to do . . . the things people in love do." Honey struggled valiantly, trying to "kill him with my knife" but he was stronger and hit her as hard as he could in the face, destroying her nose. He knocked her unconscious and "then I think he did things to me. I mean I know he did."

But the overseer paid . . . Honey waited and planned until the next cane cutting, waiting for the Black Widow Spiders to come in for shelter, placed one in a box, and empties it onto his stomach as he slept. Says Honey happily "He took a week to die. It must have hurt terribly."

Honey had learned about shells from the encyclopedia and lives comfortably collecting them for sale to an American dealer. Eventually she hopes to earn money to travel to the States for plastic surgery, and when her beauty has been restored, she want to be a call girl. "One of those girls who has a beautiful flat and lovely clothes . . . People ring them up and come and make love to them and pay for it."

Honey trusts Bond, and having given him her innermost thoughts, decides it's not quite cricket to occupy his sleeping bag by herself (he's given it to her, for the night). She tugs at his sleeve, and asks "Why don't you go to sleep . . . cold?" Bond replies that he's fine, and hears from Honey, "It's nice and warm in the sleeping-bag . . . come in? . . . Plenty of room."

Bond refuses, and is reassured by Honey's whisper, "You don't have to make love to me . . . sleep back to front, like spoons." The hero demurs gently, explaining that he is due to relieve Quarrel, but Honey extracts his promise . . . "when we get back to Jamaica."

Triumphant now, she crows, "You owe me slave time. You've promised."

Dr. No captures the two of them, and Bond tries to pass himself off as an ornithologist traveling with his wife. They're confined to an elegant prison, furnished, equipped and staffed in a grand manner.

Honey insists that Bond help her bathe ("I don't know how to work one of those places") before they eat. Bond tries desperately to keep his hands off her, and she becomes more provocative by the minute, placing both her arms round his neck while he tests the water.

"Bond's hand was on her left breast . . . her stomach pressed against his . . . why not . . . don't be a fool . . . this is a crazy time for it."

Honey teases and prods the agent, demands that he bathe her, which he manfully refuses, then play at being married.

Not at breakfast time, retorts Bond.

They finish the elaborate breakfast carried to them, and both fall into a drugged sleep.

Dr. No, their gracious host, has been just toying with Bond and Honey and decides the game has gone on long enough. Honey is to be pegged down and devoured by land crabs, while Bond is to be put through a terrifying obstacle course which leaves him battered and bruised.

After they succeed in burying Dr. No under a mountain of guano, Bond and Honey get away by themselves . . . to Honey's home. Expecting a hovel, Bond is pleasantly surprised to discover that the cellar where she lives is no hovel, and she has laid the table formally with damask cloth, gleaming silver and glassware and a tantalizing cold meal of lobster and fruit. While they are eating, Honey orders Bond to talk only of love. Tell me everything, everything you know.

"I can either eat or talk love . . . I can't do both," says Bond. Honey retorts that he will be going to Kingston the next day, and there's plenty to eat there. Talk love, she demands.

Honey Chile stood away from the table, and began to undress. First the blouse, then the skirt. She was pale in the moonlight. Taking Bond by the hand, she lifted him, and slowly, carefully removed his shirt. Her body, smelled of "new-mown-hay and sweet pepper."

On the bed, a sleeping bag lay open. Honey elaborated to Bond: "I bought this today. It's a double one. It cost a lot of money. Take those off and come in. You promised. You owe me slave time."

From Bond book to Bond book, the endless chain of Bond girls stretches. There are three contestants in Goldfinger. A lesser Dupont has been gambling with and losing to Goldfinger, and Bond is enlisted to determine his methods. He notices that Goldfinger always plays facing the hotel, and a little detective work establishes that he is being told by walky talky, what plays are required to conquer his unsuspecting partner. A swift calculation tells Bond in what room he has seen the glint of field glasses, and he rushes in to surprise Jill Masterson, a statuesque blonde of 5' 10 clad in black briefs. She is beautiful, with palest long hair, falling unfashionably long, heavily to her shoulders. Her eyes are deep blue against a lightly sunburned skin, and her mouth is bold and generous.

She follows Bond's orders to relay a message to Goldfinger, warns him not to leave the table, and to pay the minor Dupont what he has taken from him, plus Bond's fee.

That job done, Bond leaves by train for New York, and Jill Masterson is a temporary hostage. For once, there's no chase and no intruder. It had been a wonderful trip up in the train . . . to the rhythm of the giant diesels pounding out the miles, they made long, slow love in the narrow berth." . . . The girl was starved of physical love. She woke him twice more in the night with soft, demanding caresses, saying nothing, just reaching for his hard, lean body. Next day, she pulled down the roller blinds to shut out the harsh light and took him by the hand, saying, 'Love me James,' as though she were demanding candy."

No cloying farewells here, Bond had just received ten thousand dollars for saving Goldfinger's gambling victim, and he makes her take the money. "It ought to be a million," he says.

One more hard kiss and she's gone. Neither she nor Bond had "regrets," and in his mind, as he is whirled off by cab:

"Some love is fire, some love is rust. But the finest, cleanest love is lust."

A few months later, in France, Tilly Soames arrives on the scene when Bond, in an Aston Martin, is tailing Goldfinger in a Rolls. Bond notices a Triumph driven by a girl, sometimes behind him, sometimes in front, and defensively he slams on his brakes and backs up quickly. The Triumph suffers more than the Aston Martin in the collision which results. Bond walks around back of the car and notes that the girl, "her face tense with anger, had one beautiful silken leg on the road . . . providing an indiscreet glimpse of white thigh. She strips off her goggles and stands, legs apart and arms akimbo."

Chortles Bond: "If you touch me there again you'll have to marry me," and receives an open handed slap across the face. A tongue lashing follows. Bond pondered, if only pretty girls were always angry, they would be beautiful.

The girl asks frantically whether Bond will take her to Geneva, and for the first time he considered her as a pretty girl who had wanted to be picked up by Goldfinger, or to blackmail him.

There was, he thought, too much character and honesty in the face. And her uniform was hardly that of a seductress. A white, rather masculine cut, heavy silk shirt with long full sleeves was open at the neck, but could be buttoned to a military collar.

She had the unpainted fingernails we have come to look for in Bond girls, and the very wide black stitched leather belt with double brass buckles. The short pleated skirt was charcoal, and the shoes expensive looking black sandals. A pink scarf provided the only touch of color. Although it was attractive, there was something a little masculine and "open air" about her behavior and appearance, thought Bond. She could be a member of the English women's ski team, or of the horsey set.

A beautiful girl, she was the kind who lets well enough alone. "No attempt to pat her hair into place . . . it looked as a girl's hair should look — untidy with bits that strayed and an uneven parting." The hair formed an uneven, jagged dark frame for the pale face . . . blue eyes under dark brows . . . desirable mouth . . . high cheekbones and fine jaw line. A self reliant figure, body held proudly, fine breasts out thrust.

The aggressive lady introduces herself as Miss Tilly Soames, entrant in the Swiss Women's Open Championship, but Bond has his doubts. They test each other during the ride to Geneva, and Tilly disappears at the first opportunity, while Bond departs in search of Goldfinger.

As Bond prowls Goldfinger's grounds, he sees Tilly spreadeagled on the ground, training a rifle on the buildings below. "Damn and blast the silly bitch." thinks Bond, just before he leaps on her, and wrests the rifle from her arms. Tilly confesses she intends to kill Goldfinger, because her sister Jill Masterson, died in an emergency ward after he painted her gold. Tilly is convinced Goldfinger murdered her sister to take revenge for her trip with Bond.

Bond and Tilly are pulled in by Goldfinger's musclemen, and she reluctantly agrees to let Bond get on with the job he's come to do. After Bond endures cruel tortures, and regains consciousness he learns from Goldfinger that he and Tilly, already recognized as Jill's sister, will be confined to the crook's quarters, where they will "live and work and possibly, although Goldfinger has doubts about Tilly's inclinations, make love."

The captives compare notes, and Bone asks Tilly to let him call the shots. "All right then," she says ungraciously "Don't ever touch me or I shall kill you."

Goldfinger has summoned a group of gangsters to help implement his maniacal plan for robbing Fort Knox, and Bond looks with interest at an impressive specimen with the improbable name of Pussy Galore. Renowned as the tough-minded leader of a team of Lesbian cat burglars, Pussy, in her early thirties, presents a challenge to every man she encounters.

Miss Galore, beautifully dressed in a black masculine-cut suit, with a coffee coloured lace jabot has pale, Rupert Brooke good looks, with high cheekbones, a beautiful jawline, and the only violet eyes Bond has ever seen. The eyes, a true, deep shade of a pansy, beneath straight black brows and untidy black hair, look

candidly at the world. The mouth, a decisive slash of vermillion. "Bond liked the look of her, felt the sexual challenge all beautiful lesbians have for men . . .
"Amused by the uncompromising attitude that said to Goldfinger, and the others "All men are bastards and cheats. Don't try any masculine hocus on me . . . I'm in a separate league."

A quick look at Tilly Masterson, gazing at Pussy with "worshipping eyes and yearning lips," tells Bond that he's been outclassed in the competition for her favors. At a crucial point in the story, Bond and Tilly are attempting a getaway from the Goldfinger clan, and she hangs back to stay close to Pussy. "I'll be safe with her."

Above the Atlantic in a stolen BOAC jet, Bond discovers an unexpected ally in Pussy, when he receives a note from her.

The worst villains disposed of, and danger over, Pussy opens the connecting door with the next cabin and comes in, wearing nothing but a grey fisherman's jersey, barely decent in its coverage. There is no mistaking the message she delivers to Bond. "People keep asking me if I'd like an alcohol rub and I keep on saying that if anyone's going to rub me it's you, and if I'm going to be rubbed with anything it's you I'd like to be rubbed with."

Bond, without hesitattion, orders her to lock the door, remove the sweater and get into bed before she catches cold. Enjoying her new compliant role to the hilt, Pussy asks Bond whether he'll write her in Sing Sing. He bent to kiss the remarkable eyes, no longer hard, and said, "They told me you only liked women."

Explained Pussy, "I never met a man before." Then the details hurtled forth. "I come from the South. The definition of a virgin down there, is a girl who can run faster than her brother. At twelve, said Miss Galore, she was outrun by her uncle.

Bond smiles down and prescribes TLC — tender loving care.

It starts, ruthlessly, right there.

Bond's creator, Ian Fleming did a lot of type casting. With one notable exception, the Bond girls with their long heavy hair, straight noses, clearly defined jaws, wide sensuous mouths, sunburned faces with high cheekbones, athletic bodies, fine breasts, madcap driving, narrow waists cinched in wide leather belts, and demanding sexuality, follow a pattern.

Mary Ann Russel, Judy Havelock, Lisl Baum and Liz Krest, play the female lead roles in five secret occasions of Bond's life . . . all of them appear in the short story collection, For Your Eyes Only.

In Thunderball, Bond's pace is stepped up. He starts out quietly at a private hospital called "Shrublands" devoting himself solely and exclusively to getting back into shape. But there is that lovely osteopath, Patricia Fearing, and before he checks out of Shrublands, Bond has time to claim special treatment. In top notch shape, Bond troops off to Bermuda and encounters another "racy" Bond girl, Domino Vitali, behind the wheel of a Sapphire Blue MG.

Domino is the mistress of Largo, the villain Bond pursues, and he makes a date with her to disclose that Largo had been responsible for the death of her brother.

Domino had expected a little personal excitement, but she is unprepared for the exciting eroticism of getting a couple of sea egg spines in her foot, and having Bond provide first aid. Tearing his eyes away from the proud breasts in the tight bikini, Bond orders her roughly to turn over. He kneels, picks up her right foot, puts his lips to the point of the black spines and sucks . . . Some biting is called for too, but the painful spines are extracted with not too much difficulty. The effect on both of them is breath-taking, and Bond carries

Domino into the bathing hut to complete the therapy.

Later, after a nude swim . . . these Bond girls have such gorgeous bodies, they must get exposure, Bond breaks the news about Largo's involvement in the death of Domino's brother.

Largo has suitable punishment in mind for the mistress who crosses him and the agent who persuades her to do it . . . and Bond and Domino barely survive. A considerate gentleman through and through, Bond totters into Domino's hospital room, slips to the floor beside her bed, and goes to sleep with his head cradled on his arm.

The pain-wracked Domino moves her pillow to the edge of the bed, so she can see Bond at will, and closes her weary eyes. It will be sometime before either of them is in shape for a return engagement.

The Bond girls have suffered, and go on suffering. Now take Tracy La Comtesse Teresa di Vicenzo in the first pages of On Her Majesty's Secret Service. We discover Bond lying on the beach at Royale . . . he's spying on a lovely girl in a bikini. Not just girl watching, mark you, James Bond doesn't find that either necessary or pleasurable, but he is worried about her. Just as the lower rim of the setting sun touched the sea, the girl climbs to her feet, and begins to walk purposefully toward the point where sun and sea meet.

As Bond sets off in pursuit, two sinister looking fellows in belted trenchcoats set off, too, looking to an observant waiter like bad news.

Bond calls, "Hey, Tracy," she doesn't whirl, but turns slowly, and resentfully, looking at him through eyes puffed with tears, to ask what he wants.

As Bond begins to explain his concern, he is cut off abruptly by a warning from behind, and he turns to see the two professional faces, behind silver guns . . . gallantly wraps his coat around Tracy, and prepared for the worst, obeys the toughs' instructions to climb aboard the Bombard rescue craft heading for shore.

Bond knows Tracy, in the Biblical sense, as a result of his meeting with her in the Casino the previous evening. On the sentimental journey which draws him back to Casino Royale every year, Bond was at work, cleaning up at chemin de fer, when there was Tracy, the girl he had seen earlier at the wheel of a Lancia Flaminia Zagato Spyder. She had come from nowhere and was standing beside the croupier. Bond had no time to take in more than golden arms, beautiful golden face . . . brilliant blue eyes . . . shocking pink lips . . . plain white dress . . . golden hair down to her shoulders, then 'Banco'."

Everyone looked up at Tracy, to discover that, shamefully, when she loses she can't pay up. She whispers urgently to the Chef de Jeu, and his reply is a solemn shake of the head.

The cry goes up 'C'est le coup du deshonneur. Quelle honte!' Then, Bond comes to the rescue, he tosses two pearly plaques to the table; in a slightly bored tone excuses himself and points out, "Madame has forgotten that we agreed to play in partnership this evening."

Tracy, obviously grateful, prepares to leave the Casino, and coldly suggests that he come to Room 45 to claim his reward, "The most expensive piece of love of your life. It will have cost you four million francs. I hope it will be worth it."

And it was. Tracy stopped Bond's questions: "I said no conversation. Take off those clothes. Make love to me. You are handsome and strong. I want to remember what it can be like. Do anything you like. And tell me what you like and what you would like from me. Be rough with me. Treat me like the lowest whore in creation. Forget everything else. No questions. Take me."

The standard one hour later, Bond returned to his

own room, thinking briefly about Tracy and the self-demeaning, self-destructive attitudes which torture and drive her. Minutes later, he thinks "What the hell? All cats are grey in the dark," and is asleep.

Bond decides that Tracy is neurotic and at the end of her tether. Only about twenty-five, she made love with the "fervour and expertness of a girl who . . . had gone the route." It's settled. He will watch out for her

Tracy and the agent are delivered by the thugs to a giant corrugated aluminum transport truck, luxuriously appointed headquarters of big-time gangster Marc-Ange Draco, head of the Union Corse. And Draco is Tracy's father.

His spies are everywhere, evidently, because he knows all about Bond's rescue of Tracy and her pay-off, but instead of being indignant, he suggests that Bond court and marry his half-English daughter, and, incidentally, receive a personal gift, of one million pounds in gold, on the wedding day.

Tremendous mutual respect has sprung up between the two men — engaged in opposite fields — and they agree that Bond will keep an eye on Tracy, and that Draco will provide information and protection to Bond, when his work requires it.

And his work does require that he track down Ernst Stavro Blofeld, the sinister creator of SPECTRE who had escaped after organizing the whole operation.

Bond travels to an outwardly legitimate scientific research institute in the Swiss Alps, determined to unmask its head, Monsieur de Comte de Bleuville, as Blofeld.

There's not much opportunity to think of Tracy, because the superhero is occupied with ten gorgeous girls working on the project. All in the interests of extracting information, he pretends to love Ruby, the one he believes will be most useful. But all work isn't dull and "A small night wind rose up and moaned round the building, giving an extra warmth, even a certain friendship to what was no more than an act of physical passion. There was real pleasure in what they did to each other, and . . . when they lay quietly in each other's arms . . . they had done nothing wrong, no harm to each other."

Bond falls under suspicion, is suitably punished, and in appalling condition, goes through a hair-raising chase down the Alp, to fall exhausted and bleeding into the arms of Tracy, who coincidentally, just happens to be there.

Whether it's gratitude, relief, affection, or real love, Bond decides to marry Tracy. The reader eavesdrops on a number of dull, sweet little "nest building" conversations, and at ten-thirty on New Year's morning, Bond takes the plunge. He says "I do," in the British Consul General's drawing room — and means it.

But neither members of the Cult nor Bond have to go through an agonizing reappraisal of his rash move. Because a little after noon, he is a widower. Tracy has been precipitously dispatched by the villains who were after the bridegroom.

Now, the notable exception. Bond is a busy fellow. He has neither the time nor the inclination to conduct a courtship the way any ordinary mortal might. The meeting, the slow stirrings of mutual interest, the friendly conversations, the casual dating, the serious dating, the serious lovemaking, over a long period, the serious courtship and the marriage, with both partners absolutely sure of themselves and each other — have no place in Bond's adventures.

As a result, the usual Bond girl, beautiful and sensuous and sexy, is a kind of cardboard figure. Neither Bond nor the Bond fan knows her very well. They've been barely introduced when they are bare. But Vivienne Michel, heroine of The Spy Who Loved

Me, is alive and real, perhaps silly and self-centered, but she does exist.

Fleming's formula is different this time. No longer is the story told in the third person, seen by an omnipotent God surveying the adventures of an omnipotent James Bond.

The Spy Who Lover Me is told in the first person *female* by Vivienne Michel. Fleming's lame and coy explanation of the change in formula is provided in a message to his readers:

"I found what follows lying on my desk one morning. As you will see, it appears to be the first-person story of a young woman, evidently beautiful and not unskilled in the arts of love.

"According to her story, she appears to have been involved, both perilously and romantically, with the same James Bond whose secret-service exploits I myself have written from time to time.

"With the manuscript was a note signed "Vivienne Michel," assuring me that what she had written was purest truth and from the depths of her heart.

"I was much interested in this view of James Bond, through the wrong end of the telescope, so to speak, and, after obtaining clearance for certain minor infringements of the Official Secrets Act, I have much pleasure in sponsoring its publication."

By her own admission, Vivienne Michel was running away. From England, her background, the weather, a series of "untidy" and disappointing love affairs, the meagre furnishings and worn-out clothing of her London life. From the dullness, dankness, snobbery and suffocation of close horizons, and from her inability, though "quite an attractive rat, to make headway in the rat race."

When we meet her, Vivienne had run half-way round the world, from London to the rundown Dreamy Pines Motor Court, ten miles west of Lake George in the beautiful American Adirondacks. She's been employed to close up the motel at the end of the season. And after the job is done, she'll roar off again, on the tiny Vespa motor scooter, which is her passport to new places and new people.

When she gazes into the mirror, Vivienne sees "clear blue eyes, wide with surmise," brown eyelashes and eyebrows, a high, inquiring forehaed, topped by a widow's peak and tumble of "perfectly ordinary" dark brown hair, curving away to right and left in two big waves." Her age, 23; her height 5 ft. 6; her figure, good, although classmates at her English finishing school thought the behind too large, and the bra too unconfining. The cheekbones, high; the nose small; and the mouth generous, wide and sexy looking.

Vivienne Michel is a French Canadian Catholic, orphaned at eight, when her parents were killed in a wartime air crash, recalls only that she loved her father, and got on badly with her mother, was brought up by a widowed aunt.

Ian Fleming, Bond fans will recall, worshipped his father, who was killed when the author was eight.

Vivienne's aunt Florence Toussaint moved into the family house, and the girl became her ward. They got along, in fact, Vivienne "almost loved her" but she was a Protestant and Miss Michel who had been brought up a Catholic, was educated in the Ursuline Convent until the age of fifteen.

The atmosphere was stifling, and when Vivienne begged to be rescued, her aunt shipped her off to an English finishing school to counteract the Papist influence of her early years.

The heroine recalls her adolescent life in England, the European summer holidays, and the dreary social round, with rude and spotty and "totally unmasculine" young Englishmen. Her sexual initiation, in the box of a back-street movie theatre was as unsatisfactory as almost any other first experience. The young man involved, was just as stupid and fumbling and selfish as most others of his age. And, like most other girls who have determined to find out what all the fuss is about, Vivienne is left wondering whether it was worth it.

Next, she works for a handsome, blond Aryan, who starts out as a business acquaintance, then a friend, and who seems safe enough because he is passionately in love with another girl.

But when the other girl throws him over, Vivienne is called upon to comfort him, and within two weeks, they are sleeping together. And then Vivienne gets pregnant . . . and Kurt gets mad. He sends her to Zurich, for an abortion . . . the cost of which he generously covers by giving her one month's pay in lieu of notice, and an extra fifty pounds out of the goodness of his heart.

After that, Viv, who describes herself as a bird with one wing down, and the other wounded, manages to flutter back to Canada for an extended holiday. She has sold her belongings, to finance the trip and purchase a Vespa motor scooter, and travelling south from Montreal, heads into New York State, and through the Adirondacks, at the beginning of October.

She stops for the night at the Dreamy Pines Motor Court, and finds that the luxuriously appointed tourist camp is limping along, with only two overnight guests and no reservations for the final two weeks of the season.

The Phanceys, a middle aged couple who operate the place for the owner Sanguinetti, offer Viv a job for the balance of the season, and since she can use the money, she accepts. On October 13, Mr. and Mrs. Phancey leave, and Vivienne is left to turn over the keys to Mr. Sanguinetti, scheduled to arrive around noon on the 14th.

Understandably apprehensive at being alone so far

from the beaten track, Vivienne becomes doubly nervous when a storm rages, and dissolves into real terror when two "insurance men" turn up to make an inventory.

It is obvious almost immediately that the two are not like any insurance men Viv has ever seen before, and that they have questionable motives for being there. The two, with the unlikely nicknames of Sluggsy and Horror, soon reveal themselves as psychopaths, who quickly develop specific ideas for their entertainment.

Vivienne tries to break and run, and the two are just beginning to get enthusiastic about teaching her a lesson, when the door buzzer rings.

The two back off in confusion, and order Vivienne, whose breasts have just been bared by the brutal Sluggsy, to zip up, open the door, and get rid of the unwelcome guest.

At the door, wearing a dark blue belted rain coat, and a soft black hat, pulled far down, was a man "good-looking in a dark rather cruel way, with a scar showing whitely down his left cheek. Viv, whose zipper is stuck, struggles unsuccessfully to cover her bosom.

The visitor, of course, is none other than superhero James Bond, who has a flat tire, and wants a room for the night. No fool Bond. After several minutes of conversation, he realizes that something is very wrong, and insists on being given a room.

Now that the knight in shining armour has arrived, the action can begin and the villains reveal themselves. Bond saves Vivienne from death — from that fate worse than death, and from the motel fire calculated to bring a big insurance pay-off. The bad guys get theirs, and Bond and Vivienne get a shower. Well, they're both battered, bruised and grimy, and hot water has considerable therapeutic value.

They wash and dry each other, and "it was silly to wait any longer, so Bond carried Vivienne through and laid her down on the bed."

And then, recalls Viv, "he was lying beside me. His hands and his mouth were slow and electric, and his body in my arms was tenderly fierce. Afterward he told me that when the moment came I screamed. I didn't know I had. I only know that a chasm of piercing sweetness suddenly opened and drowned me and that I dug my nails into his hips to make sure of taking him with me. Then he sleepily said some sweet things and kissed me once, and his body slithered away and lay still."

The Vivienne wonders about giving herself so completely to this man, met only six hours before. But for him, she would be dead, after suffering "God knows what." "He fought for my life as it it had been his own. And then, when the dragon was dead he had taken me as his reward . . . In a few hours he would be gone — without protestations of love, without apologies or excuses. And that would be the end of that — gone, finished.

"All women love semi-rape. They love to be taken. It was his sweet brutality against my bruised body that had made his act of love so piercingly wonderful."

Wonderful from the handsome, cruel, love 'em and leave 'em Bond, anyhow.

CHAPTER VI

The Bond Villains

A Bond fan knows a villain when he sees one. And he sees a dandy in every Bond book. No need to look for the guy in the black stetson, to wonder whether the butler "might have done it" — no reader of Bond is confused about evil — he can spot the villain on first meeting, sometimes before James Bond himself has read the signs.

A Bond villain is inevitable non-*WASP and usually grotesque. If his natural deformities are not enough, he supplements them with spine chilling mechanical aids. Scratch a Bond villain, and you'll find a slob. Even as they are plotting the demise of James Bond, most of the villains act with exaggerated courtesy and consideration, but there is always a tell-tale sign of their boorishness.

It's in Casino Royale that we meet Le Chiffre, Soviet agent and head of a French, communist controlled trade union. Until Bond, assigned to discredit him, interferes with his plans for pulling off a big gambling win, Le Chiffre doesn't seem particularly villainous. But hell hath no fury like a villain discredited and this one emerges as diabolical.

Just after Bond receives his assignment, we get the opportunity to see Le Chiffre's dossier. The name itself is significant, meaning cypher. Le Chiffre was first observed as a displaced person, inmate of Dachau camp, in U. S. occupied Germany, 1945. He was apparently suffering from amnesia and paralysis of the vocal cords — perhaps both complaints were feigned. The dumbness was cleared up by therapy, but the subject continued to claim total loss of memory except associations with Alsace Lorraine and Strasbourg, where he was transferred on Stateless Passport No. 304 - 596. Since he was only "a number on a passport," he adopted the name Le Chiffre.

*WASP — White Anglo Saxon Protestant — the *only* thing for a snob to be.

Le Chiffre's description reveals a rather ordinary man, of impeccable sartorial taste. Height 5 ft. 8 inches, weight 18 stones. Pale complexion, clean shaven, reddish brown hair. Very dark eyes with whites showing all 'round iris. Small, rather feminine mouth. Small ears with large lobes (indicating some Jewish blood, claims the dossier). Small, well tended hirsute hands. Small feet. Racially, subject is probably a mixture of Mediterranean with Prussian or Polish strains. Dresses well and meticulously, generally in dark blue double breasted suits. Smokes incessantly, Caporals, with a denicotinizing holder. Voice soft and even. Biligual in French and English. Good German. Smiles infrequently.

The Villain's habits are characterized as expensive and discreet. He has large sexual appetites, and is a flagellant. An expert driver of fast cars, he is also adept with small arms and other instruments of personal combat. Always accompanied by two armed guards, one French, one German.

Aha, said the reader — he's no slob. But he is. Le Chiffre makes frequent and flagrant use of a benzedrine inhaler — no matter where he happens to be at the time.

Le Chiffre, it seems, either to line his pockets, or to increase his union's money, engaged speculation with union funds, borrowing some fifty million francs to purchase control of a chain of brothels. Very shortly after he acquired the holdings, the French government whimsically passed legislation closing down all the brothels in the country, and the bottom fell out of the brothel market. Le Chiffre, then, was hardpressed to find the money to return to his union funds.

He decides, as have other petty pilferers, to borrow 25 million francs, the remaining capital of the Union, and to win another fifty million at Baccarat at Eaux-les-Royales.

The British plan is for Bond, bolstered by sufficient funds, to out gamble and discredit Le Chiffre, and at the same time bankrupt that communist controlled union.

From the beginning, Bond's opposition is expecting him. Le Chiffre tries to prevent trouble before it starts by arranging a bomb throwing, but the wily Bond isn't put out of commission.

After a harrowing baccarat battle between Bond and Le Chiffre, Bond wins all, and Le Chiffre kidnaps Bond's No. 2 girl, and the agent himself — in a last-ditch attempt to relieve Bond of his winnings.

Just as Bond is suffering the tortures of the damned — damned by Le Chiffre, anyhow, a SMERSH killer arrives to dispose of Le Chiffre, who has caused no end of trouble. Like horses with blinkers, these SMERSH types — because he has no orders to dispose of Bond, he lets him live, after carving a Russian letter, denoting "spy" on the back of Bond's hand.

In Live and Let Die, Bond's encounter is with a kind of double villain — a known gangster and member of SMERSH whose activities help to finance Soviet espionage in the United States.

Bond starts on the trail of Mr. Big after M has ascertained his complete recovery from the tortures of his last adventure. A trickle of gold coins, minted prior to 1650, has appeared in the United States. They may be part of the treasure accumulated by some of the old pirates, Bloody Morgan in particular. Somehow these coins are being carried into the U. S., probably by a yacht travelling from Jamaica through the Florida Keys to St. Petersburg. It's owner is a negro gangster, whose permanent residence is Harlem.

Not content to be just a successful gangster, Mr. Big is the head of the Black Widow Voodoo cult, and believed by members of that group to be the zombie of Baron Samedi, the Price of darkness.

Mr. Big got his name from his initials (Buonaparte Ignace Gallia) and from his size.

The highly intelligent villain looms 6 ft. 6 inches, and weights 20 stone. Half French and half negro, he was born in Haiti, and was initiated into voodoo as a child. He started an underground voodoo temple in Harlem, and his pose as the Zombie of Baron Samedia holds thousands of minor villains who work for him in the grip of fear.

Prior to the war, Mr. Big developed an impressive criminal organization in New York, and ruthlessly proceeded to eliminate any opposition. He heeded the call of his country in 1943, and, despite his recod as petty gangster, was trained and utilized by the OSS. He dropped from sight for five years after the war, and may have been in Moscow, and in 1950, Mr. Big returned to Harlem with a bottomless bag of funds, and got back into business with a chain of brothels.

When Bond meets him, Big is on top of the world. Washington knows about him, but can't prove a thing. Even the old ploy of income tax evasion wouldn't work. His negro minions are terrified of him, but no one would try to kill him. He's a zombie, after all, and there'd be no point in that.

Through the eyes of a captive Bond, Mr. Big looks like this:

"It was a great football of a head, twice the normal size and very nearly round. The skin was grey-black, taunt and shining like the face of a week-old corpse in the river (appropriate for a zombie, actually). It was hairless, except for some grey-brown fluff above the ears. There were no eyebrows and no eyelashes and the eyes were extraordinarlily far apart so that one could not focus on them both, but only one at a time. Their gaze was very steady and penetrating. When they rested on something they seemed to devour it, to encompass the whole of it. They bulged slightly and the irises were golden round black pupils which were now wide. They were animal eyes, not humans and they seemed to blaze."

Well, violence begets violence, and after Bond has

maddened Mr. Big because he innocently attracts the villain's ward, Solitaire — and interferes with the smooth operation of his enterprises; tortures and sadism abound. Even poor Felix Leiter is dropped through a trapdoor into a tank containing a man-eating shark. In the end though, Mr. Big gets his, in a most unzombie like way.

Bond fans were startled by the Moonraker because at first sight, the villain seems to be an internationally renowned Englishman, and that would never do.

"M" summons Bond to discuss what he terms a personal matter, and asks Bond to help him out — perhaps an evening should be enough. Bond is startled then, when "M" asks him what he knows of Sir Hugo Drax, whose name is on the front page of every newspaper, and aired on every newsbroadcast. Bond's summary goes like this:

"The man's a national hero. The public have taken to him . . . Theyv'e got a real feeling for him . . . consider he's one of them, but a glorified version. A sort of superman. He's not much to look at, with all those scars from his war injuries, and he's a bit loud-mouthed and ostentatious. But they rather like that . . . They like his friends calling him "Hugger" Drax. It makes you think what he's doing for the country, out of his own pocket, and far beyond what any government seems able to do . . . it's extraordinary . . . they don't insist on making him Prime Minister."

Drax has cornered the market on Columbite, a valuable ore with an extraordinarily high melting point. Jet engines can't be manufactured without it, and it's hard to come by, with only a few thousand tons produced every year, as a by-product of the Nigerian tin mines.

After methodically building a multi-million dollar empire, Drax decided to reveal his contribution to the country, directly to the Queen. His letter, beginning

"Your majesty, may I have the temerity . . ." outlined his intention to give his entire holding in Columbite to Britain, to build a super atomic rocket with a range that would cover nearly every capital in Europe. An immediate and effective answer to anyone who tried to atom-attack London.

The designs, the staff, and the testing were to be financed by Drax' personal contribution of ten million pounds . . . after months of debate and investigation, a grateful Queen accepted on behalf of the people of Britain, and conferred a knighthood on the resourceful philanthropist, Drax.

Now, for the shocker — "Sir Hugo Drax cheats at cards."

"M" is a member of the Blades, a gambling club hoary with tradition and gentlemanly behavior, and he is sick with the knowledge of Sir Hugo's cheating. Will Bond confirm the fact of his cheating, and expose him? That would be the only discreet way of handling the problem.

Drax too, gave the impression of being a little larger than life. "He was physically big, about six feet, with exceptionally broad shoulders, topped by a big square head, with tight reddish hair parted in the middle. On either side, the hair line curved down toward the temples, probably to hide the shining puckered skin, that covered most of the right half of the face. Other signs of plastic surgery could be seen in the right ear, not a perfect match for the left; and the bloodshot right eye, which was a surgical disaster. It was much larger than the left, as a result of a contraction of the borrowed skin used to rebuild the upper and lower eyelids.

Concealing as much of the lower face as possible, were a bushy reddish moustache, sideburns down to the bottom of the earlobes, and patches of hair on the cheekbones.

The heavy moustache also served to conceal the protruding upper teeth, and the fang-like "centrals", until Drax gave his short braying laugh.

The general effect of the face was flamboyant. Rather, Bond thought like a circus ringmaster.

"A bullying, boorish, loud-mouthed vulgarian. That would have been Bond's verdict if he had not known something of Drax's abilities. As it was, it crossed his mind that much of the effect might be Drax's idea of a latter-day Regency buck — the harmless disguise of a man with a smashed face, who was also a snob.

Well, the Moonraker project is important, and Bond is assigned by Security to move in after the shooting death of the first Security agent.

With the help of Gala Brand, Bond discovers that the project smells to high heaven, and that Drax, the villainous Englishman is really an ultra-villainous German, pathological in his hatred of Britain, and determined to aim the Moonraker squarely at London.

He was, the Bond fan realizes, far too horible to be an Englishman.

The notorious American gangsters Bond takes on single handed in Diamonds are Forever, shape up more like small-time Hollywood producers of B movies. They have funny names — Jack and Seraffimo Spang — and funny hobbies. Seraffino is steeped in the legend of the old west . . . bought himself a ghost town in Nevada, and an old Western locomotive and early Pullman state coach, and spends his weekends playing trains in a big way.

"Mr. Spang was dressed in full Western costume down to the long silver spurs on his polished black boots. The costume, and the broad leather chaps that covered his legs were in black, picked and embellished with silver. The big quiet hands rested on the ivory butts of two long barrelled revolvers which protruded from a holster down each thigh, and the broad black belt from which they hung was ribbed with ammunition."

Far more in keeping with the traditional repulsiveness of the Bond villain, are a couple of supporting actors in Diamonds are Forever, Wint and Kidd, the two "fingermen" who move ominously through the book and toward Bond. One is "youngish, with a pretty white face, and prematurely white hair. The other has the consistency of a rice pudding, his face "has the glistening, pasty appearance of a spat out bullseye."

Dr. No, as Fleming wrote him, is inscrutable and ageless in the most villainous oriental tradition.

When Bond receives his briefing from 'M", he discovers that the man who calls himself Dr. Julius No is half Chinese, half German, and has upset the American Audobon Society because of his carelessness about preservation of the Roseate Spoonbills which had found sanctuary on guano island.

Bond, held captive in elegantly comfortable surroundings, finally comes face to face with Dr. No.

"His first impression is of thinness and erectness and height." Bond himself is more than six feet, and Dr. No towers at least six inches over him, "but the straight, immovable poise of his body made him seem still taller. The head was also elongated and tapered from a round, completely bald skull down to a sharp chin . . . the impression was of a reversed raindrop . . . oildrop, for the skin was of a deep almost translucent yellow."

It was impossible to calculate Dr. No's age, for there were no lines in face, or forehead. The eyebrows were Dali-esque-fine, black and upswept sharply, as though they had been painted on. Slanting jet black eyes without lashes . . . unblinking and devoid of expression, stared out. A thin fine nose ended abruptly above a wide "compressed wound of a mouth" cruel, authoritative, permanently fixed in a hint of a smile. The chin receded toward the neck, rarely moving away from centre, creating the impression that head and spine were one.

"The bizarre, gliding figure looked like a giant venomous worm wrapped in gray tin-foil, and Bond would have not been surprised to see the rest of it trailing slimily along the carpet.

Dr. No apologizes for not shaking hands, and reveals two pairs of steel pincers concealed in the sleeves of his kimona.

Relishing the revulsion with which Bond and Honeychile have greeted him, Dr. No indulges himself in icing the cake by warning them that his eyes see everything, and emphasizing the point by tapping them delicately with one of the steel claws. He wears contacts, you see.

Dr. No reveals that he is a victim of the Tong wars, who rebuilt his body, created a new character, and devoted years to the study of the human mind and the body.

"Because I wished to know what this clay is capable of. I had to learn what my tools were before I put them to use on my next goal — total security from physical weaknesses."

His aim, the achievement of power — to treat others as he had been treated — the power to give life or death to decide, to judge, the power of absolute independence from outside authority.

Bond, we know, already has this kind of power. But he's British, after all, and on the side of right, so there's nothing reprehensible about his omnipotence.

Dr. No is mad, you see, and Bond tells him so. "The only difference is that instead of being shut up, you've built your own asylum and shut yourself up in it."

Guano mining though, is just Dr. No's means of financing his primary interest, sabotaging American guided missile tests. He's in partnership with Russia now, but is already considering switching his allegiance to Red China which may cough up more money.

All in the interests of science, Dr. No proposes to

subject Bond and Honey to a lot of torture. "I shall record the length of your endurance. The facts will be noted. One day my findings will be given to the world. Your deaths will have served the purposes of science, I never waste human material."

But evil must be punished, and Dr. No, in a kind of divine retribution at the hands of superhero Bond, goes to a gasping, choking, suffocating death under tons of guano.

At the opposite end of Bond's villainy scale is Auric Goldfinger, about five feet high, and so out of proportion that he might have been put together with pieces of other peoples bodies. He has a moon shaped face, and an enormous round head. Everything about him is golden — the name, the sun tanned skin, the carrotty hair on his head and chest. His car is bright yellow — pure gold, we learn later — and he keeps much of his wealth in gold bars with him all the time. A typically acquisitive greedy grasping, Jewish financier, the bigots would say.

He gets his sexual kicks from painting his girls yellow, and even uses the technique to dispose of one of them he believes has betrayed him.

His ultimate villainy is an attempt to rob Fort Knox.

Goldfinger's chauffeur-bodyguard is a charmer, too. A huge Korean named Oddjob, whose cleft palate makes him impossible to understand. Oddjob makes up for his speech impediment by being an expert in karate, so accomplished and practiced that he has grown ridges of bonelike tissue down the edge of each hammy hand. He demonstrates his ability by way of warning Bond, when he splits a six by four polished oak banister with a couple of apparently effortless chops.

Then there's Blofeld, the man who created SPECTRE. Bond meets him three times in Thunderball, On Her Majesty's Secret Service and You Live Only Twice.

Blofeld is one villain who evidently delights in playing Doctor. In On Her Majesty's Secret Service, his objective is infecting British agriculture with crop and livestock pests, carried by a group of innocently involved agricultural workers he has treated for "allergies" in his Swiss Alps sanitorium.

Still waiting for his first glimpse of Blofeld, Bond gets a look at the waiters in the mountain retreat.

"There were twelve of them in sight. It was not difficult to sum them up as three Corsicans, three Germans, three vaguely Balkan faces, Turks, Bulgars or Yugoslavs, and three obvious Slavs. There would probably be three Frenchmen in the kitchen."

The original Blofeld, blackmailing Western Governments by threatening to hijack nuclear bombs, in Thunderball was "about twenty stone, tall, pale, bland faced with a black crew cut, black eyes with whites all round, ugly thin mouth, long pointed hands and feet." Chameleon-like, he had changed by the time he established his clinic in the Alps, and assumed the identity of Monsieur Le Comte de Bleuville. Still tall, with long hands and feet, this time, he had long, carefully tended fine silver hair. His ears, previously close to his head, protruded slightly, and the heavy body had reduced to not more than twelve stone, with no signs of the sagging flesh which usually accompanies such drastic reduction.

The mouth was full and friendly, with a pleasant disconcertingly steady smile. The forehead was wrinkled, above a nose which had been short and squat and was now aquiline, marred by what might have been the ravaging effects of a syphilitic eating away around the right nostril. The eyes were opaque dark green pools — contact lenses again.

We learned in Thunderball that Blofeld had been born in "Gdynia," of a Polish father and Greek mother. Early in his career he travelled to Sweden, Turkey and South America, a member of a kind of villainous jet set, juggling stolen funds which left him wealthy after careful investment.

Blofeld is paranoid and maniacal in his lust for power, but he's an efficient villain who delegates responsibility for much of the detailed work to his loyal underlings.

In From Russia With Love, Donovan Grant, now Krassno Granitsky, is an Irishman gone wrong — clear over to Russia, that is, where his passion for killing at the time of the full moon, is a marketable commodity. He is the Chief Executioner of SMERSH.

"He was the result of a midnight union between a German professional weight lifter and a Southern Irish waitress . . . for a quarter of an hour on the damp grass behind a circus tent out side Belfast."

But to Bond — and to Bond fans, there's really no villain like the female villain. In an earlier century, they would have been considered witches.

Colonel Rosa Klebb is a doll, toad like, middle aged, short and dumpy, the bulge of uniform like a badly packed sandbag. Her face is in keeping with her personality "Thinning orange hair scraped back to a tight obscene bun, . . . a wedge of thickly powdered large pored nose; the wet rap of a mouth . . . pale, thick chicken's skin that scragged in little folds under the ears and at the corners of the mouth . . . big peasant's ears. And besides everything else, Rosa stinks, and tries to cover it with cheap scent.

She'll allow, it's rumoured in Moscow, no torture to take place until she can attend . . . and arrives, like the "tricoteuses of the French Revolution," bearing her handy little stool, to watch with relish.

It's Rosa Klebb, disguised as a proper lady, who gives Bond that nearly fatal kick in the shins at the end of from Russia with Love. A poisoned blade concealed in the toe of her pointed shoe, does the trick . . . in a last grand gesture before Rosa is carted off for punishment.

Through every book, every villain emerges as something of magnificent evil. The fact that they may stink or be physically deformed, or suffer the ultimate dignity of not being British, is incidental to the overall fact that in every case the villian is larger than life.

But then, what other type of enemy could there before a super hero who was, himself, so much larger than life.

CHAPTER VII

Sadism, Masochism And James Bond

The critics screamed bloody blue murder, the self-styled protectors of present-day morality declared through clenched teeth and quickened breathing that the Bond books were corrupting our youth and stimulating crimes of violence.

And through it all James Bond was captured, and bound up, and beaten and bloodied and tortured. He screamed and fainted and vomited, but always came through.

The Bond-girls, passionate and palpitating to be in the embrace of the Superhero, had their share of violence, too. They were stripped naked, and threatened with the ultimate indignities and obscenities by a chain of revolting minor villains. They were slapped, and punched, and tied down, spreadeagled and tortured with fiery cigarettes and chilling icecubes, but they came through, too, at least until they could enjoy the ultimate ecstacy of exalted lovemaking with Bond. And then, if necessary, they died with smiles on their faces.

In The Spy Who Loved Me, Vivienne endures a particularly brutal beating at the hands of her two tough-guy captors.

She describes, with scarcely masked masochistic delight, how "slowly, almost caressingly, he began to hit me." As the beating went on, her tormentor was "choosing his targets with refined, erotic cruelty."

When it was over, Vivienne came to in the shower. She was lying naked among the remnants of her torn clothing. As she climbed to her knees, her reported reaction was not of pain or anger or humiliation. Instead, she says, "I was a tamed, whimpering animal. I retched."

With a touching display of understanding and a philosophical air, the thug who had beaten her up suggests that she go ahead and be sick. Patting her on the bottom, he says "Go ahead baby. First thing after a beat-up, everyone vomits." She vomits.

In From Russia With Love, Bond's host invites him to attend a special fight. Two women will fight all out with the winner getting the man both love.

Zora, the bigger of the two had things going pretty much her way through the fight until Vida, ignoring the Marquis of Queensbury in favor of the Marquis de Sade, buries her face in the massive, nude breasts of the big woman.

". . . Her teeth were at work." As her teeth gnawed, Vida's hands worked too, her nails ripped at the exposed skin of the other woman through the torn clothes.

When the two combatants backed away, they moved like cats, "their shining bodies glinting through the last rags of their shifts and blood showing on the exposed breasts of the big girl."

Bondage appears over and over as Bond and friends are trussed, tied and staked out for an assortment of painful pastimes.

In Casino Royale, Bond takes the seat of honor in a chair with the bottom cut away so that the lower part of his body is conveniently exposed. Fleming's careful attention to detail describes the position quite clearly.

"The thin man produced some flex. With this he bound Bond's wrists to the arms of the chair and his ankles to the front legs. He passed a double strand across his chest, under the arm-pits and through the chair-back. He made no mistake with the knots and left no play in any of the bindings. All of them bit sharply into Bond's flesh."

Fleming reminds us again at this point that Bond was naked and defenseless, "his buttocks and the underpart of his body protruded through the chair."

The evil Le Chiffre dismissed his helper and casually lit a cigarette as he sat in front of the helpless, naked Bond. As he sits, the tormentor picks up a twisted cane carpet-beater and places it so that it leans against his knee with the base under the exposed Bond.

When, with a quick move of his wrist, he strikes the top of the beater, the instrument moves sharply under Bond's chair with the cut-away bottom.

"Bond's whole body arched in an involuntary spasm." He suffers through a long paragraph of sweating, soundless screaming, finger and toe clenching and body sagging before "he uttered a deep groan."

In Thunderball, sadism takes on a humanitarian cloak when Domino steps on sea eggs which bury ugly black spines in her foot. When Bond picked up her right foot to minister to it, he brushed away the sand to see the rose-like qualities of the toes.

Holding back the toes and pressing his lips against the broken ends of the spines, "he sucked hard for about a minute." While this removed some of the foreign matter which he spat out, it is not sufficient.

He informs Domino that unless he hurts her a bit it will take a long time ". . . and I can't waste too much time over just one foot."

"Bond sunk his teeth into the flesh . . ." When he paused to spit out the fragments he had sucked from the wound, he saw the marks left by his teeth. He licked away the blood before remarking, "This is the first time I've eaten a woman. They're rather good."

In Dr. No, Bond discovers the art of confinment and torture without a blow being struck. As a centipede crawls along his leg, he knows that even the slightest movement on his part could cause the creature to make its death dealing bite.

It moves slowly so that Bond has a lot of time to think. As it moves toward his groin, as of course it must, Bond wonders if it will find the warmth there interesting enough to decide on a snack. Will it, he wonders, try to crawl into the crevices?

After a lengthy tour of the Bond anatomy, the centipede leaves without biting. Only then does the man move. It is his turn now and he kills the intruder with much squishing and oozing and crunching.

When, in You Only Live Twice, an unfortunate man falls into a lake populated by deadly piranna, "Their six-inch bodies glittered and flashed in the moonlight . . . Once the man raised his head and let out a single, terrible scream and Bond saw that his face was encrusted with pendant fish."

Only after the muderous minnows have dined on his jugular does the unfortunate Herr Doktor stop fighting. With no apparent regret, Fleming sums up the situation with, ". . . had certainly provided a feast . . . unending dishes for their delectation! A true banquet of death!"

In the wonderful world of James Bond, even the fish enjoy gourmet tastes.

CHAPTER VIII

The Bond Cult

In order to obtain some insight into the Bond phenomenon, the authors talked to a group of nine intelligent young Bond afficianados and one devil's advocate.

The discussion which follows is the product of that meeting. None of the people present worked at attaining objectivity — their conversation was heated and fraught with emotional overtones. Frequently they shouted, at each other or merely in order to be heard — and Roberts Rules of Order just did not apply.

Bond fans or not, they were involved in the discussion, and in Bond. As you will see from the transcript, for them, James Bond the superhero and Ian Fleming the author were synonymous. They frequently used "Bond" when they meant Fleming . . . and in discussing Fleming, they used the present tense, rather than the past tense, as though they had not accepted the fact of his death.

If he did nothing else, Fleming succeeded in making Bond live for his readers. Even the anti-Bond contributor was vehement in her dislike of him.

And sometimes, too, the afficianados began their discussion liking the Bond books for one reason, and ended it, contradicting themselves, and liking them for another. Sometimes they appeared to rationalize their admiration of Bond and his adventures, as though the criticism of Fleming and his works had made them self-conscious about their devotion to him.

INTERVIEWER I: Bob, you helped recruit this group of James Bond fans for us tonight. And you're a James Bond fan yourself. Have you read all the books?

BOB: Every one, including a collection of short stories.

INTERVIEWER I: Have you read Thrilling Cities, you know, the travel thing Fleming did a few years ago?

BOB: No, I haven't read that one.

LYNN: That wasn't nearly so good as the Bond books. There was no comparison.

INTERVIEWER I: Why do you like James Bond?

BRAD: First, I find the books very entertaining. They read quickly — don't give you anything to sit and think about. There are no weighty paragraphs to be pondered. I can't just launch into a speech about why *I* find them so entertaining — I'd like to comment further after we've heard from someone else. I've seen the films, too.

INTERVIEWER I: The films are really an entirely different phenomenon, in my opinion. It's one thing to go to a movie house and sit watching the screen, where magnificent scenery, beautiful colour, gorgeous girls and great gadgetry completely entertain you, and it's another thing to pick up the first book, become interested in it, interested enough to buy the second and third and fourth and fifth.

BRAD: Isn't this what they're working on in the films? I think there's a great similarity between the Bond films and the Bond books. The films are in colour alright, but so are the books. Your imagination is sparked by this kind of copy — everybody has a picture in his mind when he reads these books. There's a lot of colour.

INTERVIEWER I: Is the picture dispelled or shaken at all when you see a film? Is Sean Connery what you thought James Bond would be?

BRAD: It's like a radio announcer. When you hear a radio announcer on the air, he's never what you think he looks like.

(LAUGHTER) *A WELL KNOWN RADIO ANNOUNCER WAS PRESENT*. No, John will back me up.

BRAD: (continuing) No, I wasn't at all disappointed in the films. The thing that disappointed me most of all about James Bond were the critics, and the people who said, "It's all escapism," and I was sitting there enjoying it.

INTERVIEWER I: Escaping.

BRAD: (continuing) (going on, not catching the significance of the last remark) Yes, "escapism and it's a mass catharthis —

MARJORIE: (breaking in) It's wish fulfillment.
BRAD: A purging of many things. And here I was enjoying it, not knowing or caring why, and I felt suddenly guilty. They were telling me, "You shouldn't enjoy this, it's terrible, you're some kind of a slob.
BOB: It's capitalistic propaganda.
BRAD: I was reading it and liking it, and then I felt guilty about it and didn't read anymore.
INTERVIEWER I: I talked today to a psychologist who said this is everyman's dream. James Bond is living everyman's dream.
BRAD: Sure.
MARJORIE: That's a terrible thing to think — that this is everyman's dream.
BRAD: You should be a man for awhile, honey, you'd love it.
INTERVIEWER I: The psychologist said, James Bond is invincible.
LYNN: That's right, he always comes out on top.
BOB: Literally.
LYNN: That matters a lot.
INTERVIEWER I: He's licensed to kill. Everybody likes to think that he could destroy his enemies. Bond is licensed to kill. And I said, okay what about his sexual adventures, there's no emotional involvement, Bond says "How do you do, bang!" The answer was that that, too is everyman's dream.
ROSS: Bond's sexual prowess, the way that Fleming has written it, is really not the best that's on the market, you can get much more hairy stuff, but Fleming I think went along on one theory. He's had his little moments in life, and Bond should have his moments. Bond's women were probably much more gorgeous than the ones Fleming ever played kissy face with, but the thing is he (Fleming) gave the guy that — he was able to go out and have a fling.
BOB: He was a playboy.

LYNN: And also he's made it alright. He's excused the females involved.
BOB: It's Hefner all the way to the Nth.
BRAD: Excused, what do you mean, excused?
MARJORIE: It's expediency.
LYNN: We're not talking about morals, are we. He's excused it, there's reason for it.
MARJORIE: How can anyone sit back and admire a man who is a cad, a sadist.
BOB: How? It's easy as hell. You just project yourself into it, that's all.
BRAD: Because you can't do it.
BOB: Easy, easy, *you* can't.
MARJORIE: I think Bond is wish fulfillment.
BRAD: Wish fulfillment? I wish I could be like him. Right.
MARJORIE: Do you really?
BRAD: Well how many of us wouldn't like to be like Bond?
MARJORIE: If you do, I think it's awfully sad.
LYNN: I'd like to meet somebody like Bond.
JOHN: I'd love to be like Bond.
BRAD: When you get down to Bond's sex life. Don't forget in one of his books, this boy has decided, okay, here's a very fine girl called whatshername whatsername, and he's driving along in a Porsche or something and Count Whathisname comes along beside him, it's the end of the book, and he shoots them. And they went off the road, and she died. And that was Bond's big love, and she died.
INTERVIEWER I: Well, that was the point.
BRAD: You see, it's not always for expediency, and there's an excuse for it, he liked it.
LYNN: What's wrong with it?
INTERVIEWER I: We're not talking about what's wrong with it, we're talking about what makes it interesting for some people and not at all interesting for

others. It's been our experience that it's been very hard to find women who are Bond fans. There were a number of men.

CAROL: It just depends on whether you want to identify with Bond or with his woman of the moment.

BOB: His playmate.

BRAD: When you read a book do you put yourself in the part of the female?

CAROL: No, not when I'm escaping.

MARJORIE: Not when I'm escaping, I do it of course when I read a psychological novel or something, but I don't as far as my escapism goes.

INTERVIEWER I: Do you read murder mysteries, Marjorie?

MARJORIE: Yes.

INTERVIEWER I: You like murder mysteries and spy stories, but you don't like these particular ones.

MARJORIE: I don't like these at all.

INTERVIEWER I: Do you actively dislike them or are you just indifferent to them?

MARJORIE: No, I'm not at all indifferent, I really heatedly dislike them. Maybe this is a clue to me. But I think it's appalling that Bond should be the dream of most of the men I meet.

BRAD: No, please it's not the dream.

BOB: There's an envy thing in here.

BRAD: I like champagne, the worst thing that could happen to me is to have champagne all the time.

LYNN: Doesn't everybody have champagne all the time?

BRAD: Oh no, you've got to have brandy and a cube of sugar with it sometimes. I recommend that you ride on the Leaside bus, because Seagrams have a thing on the wall, "Moderation is the key to success." When you read one of these, it's exciting, man is an adventurous animal.

MARJORIE: Bond — that's what he is, he's an animal.

He doesn't think —
BRAD: He calculates his moves very carefully.
INTERVIEWER I: Is Bond intelligent?
MARJORIE: No.
BOB: He operates at a gonad level.
MARJORIE: As I say, he's a cad. He can't think. He's unintelligent. He's a snob. He's horribly, horribly pretentious.
INTERVIEWER I: Is he a snob, or is he just British?
BOB: Ian Fleming has created a Bond character. This is not somebody writing a book.
MARJORIE: Oh James Bond is Ian Fleming's wish fulfillment as much as he's yours or yours.
BRAD: Oh now look, don't get me wrong.
ROSS: I think that Fleming has given Bond a little bit of the slightly upper middle class English way of life, and over here we would consider it snobbish, and over there its alright. Where you may have a handkerchief shoved up your sleeve.
MARJORIE: Okay, I've read a lot of English fiction, and I have a background there, and I think I can distinguish between snobbery per se and the English middle class way.
LYNN: He's not snobbish.
ROSS: I don't think it's snobbery to come out with good wines. This is the league you're in.
MARJORIE: Those abominable drinks that he drinks.
BOB: Abominable!
MARJORIE: I wouldn't drink them.
BRAD: That doesn't make them abominable.
LYNN: But I happen to like these drinks, and I happen to like his food. I don't object to him in any way. I don't think he's snobbish, I think that he's living the life that his salary and his job are giving him.
INTERVIEWER II: What about his attitude toward anyone who is not British? Are not all his villains non-English?

LYNN: Yes, but it's the same way with American writers.

BRAD: It has to be.

LYNN: You know that bad cowboys always wear black stetsons, and all the good ones wear white. You have to distinguish somehow. And I think when you're writing at any period, you have to pick out who is then the villain in world affairs and you put them forward. For the last number of year's it's been the Russians.

MARJORIE: But if you're speaking about British spy stories, what about "Our Man in Havana" or Somerset Maugham's "Ashendon."

ROSS: That was an excellent book.

BRAD: What about "The Spy Who Came in From the Cold."?

LYNN: That was just beautiful.

MARJORIE: Here was not a cardboard, one dimensional character. Here's a man. It's not a spy story, it's a novel and a very good one.

LYNN: But James Bond is much more entertaining to read. And offers much more escapism.

BOB: I found "The Spy Who Came In From The Cold" actually much better reading than most of the Bond books.

LYNN: Yes, but there aren't enough of them, there are only one or two or three.

BRAD: He's a depressing bugger.

LYNN: There are lots of Bond books that you can keep reading.

BOB: "The Spy Who Came In From the Cold" was written by the ultimate civil servant who finally rebelled, and wrote this kind of book.

LYNN: Well, although I liked him, I didn't really relate to that man in "The Spy Who Came In From the Cold."

INTERVIEWER I: Do you relate to James Bond?

LYNN: Well, I'd like to. I really would.

MARJORIE: What's the difference between liking to and relating?
BOB: She is a female.
LYNN: Well, unfortunately, "The Spy Who Came In" is much more the sort of person I'm going to meet. But I would really like to meet somebody like James Bond.
INTERVIEWER II: What is the charm of Bond?
LYNN: He drinks champagne.
INTERVIEWER: So does the bartender at the club.
LYNN: He's at home in any situation. He can fit into any situation ,and he can talk about anything, and he knows his way around, and he dresses well and properly, drives the right car.
ROSS: And the average guy cannot do it.
MARJORIE: All these things are superficial.
INTERVIEWER: The average guy cannot afford to do it?
ROSS: Not so much cannot afford to do it. There's a lot of criticism comes at men, because they may have all the money but they behave like absolute boors, or they don't know how to make the first move toward a woman. Bond always smacks of a little bit of finesse. Even at the right time, the author has built you up to a stage where there's only one thing that he's got to do to her. You know it, Bond knows it, and we're all hoping that she knows it, and invariably it's carried through with finesse. I think what Fleming is putting across is that this is the elegant way that Bond pursues his women.
INTERVIEWER I: Is Bond a masculine character?
ROSS: (goes right on) Bond is always couth. He's never uncouth.
INTERVIEWER I: He knows which is the right fork?
ROSS: Not only that, but he knows the way the lady wants to be received at that right time. (sic) In this case, I would have to say that I as an individual am the most miserable duffer.

LYNN: Oh sweetie, you always do the right thing.
BRAD: And it's hard to cut my sirloin steak with my fish knife.
ROSS: I think the Bond books have a lot of appeal for a woman, in that she sees a type of man that just is not around. Now and again they may be around, but let's face it, in our normal lot of life, very rarely.
MARJORIE: But Ross, a normal woman wouldn't want this sort of a man.
LYNN: I would.
BOB: You'd better believe it!
BRAD: It's a short life.
LYNN: One thing I love about Bond is that he puts . . .
ROSS: Nowhere in all these novels does Jimmy Bond pick his nose. Nowhere. And Marjorie, I know you would hate to be sitting opposite a guy at dinner, and he's busy going like this (gesturing).
LAUGHTER. You wouldn't even look at him.
CAM: She looks at me.
ROSS: That's different, you're married to her.
LYNN: Always with finesse.
MARJORIE: In From Russia With Love Kerim wins this gypsy girl in a fight, she's fighting him all the way, resisting him, so eventually he takes her home with him, chains her naked under a table, naked, and I gather, kicks her or beats her whenever she dares to struggle.
ROSS: I've got to read that book again.
MARJORIE: And Bond admires this, that's the sort of thing he admires.
LYNN: It wasn't in the book I read.
ROSS: Well, that's the lustful way.
LYNN: What other way is there?
INTERVIEWER I: Both Bond and Ian Fleming are quoted as saying women should never have been given the vote.
LYNN: The one thing I really do feel about Ian Flem-

ing's writing, the reason I like him, is that he puts the man into the position where the man would really like to be. Most men would like to be like James Bond. Be able to order the fine things, do the right things, lay the right girls. The whole bit.

BOB: Oh! You might say seduce, but go ahead.

LYNN: Okay, seduce. And he does the same thing with females, he gives you the freedom. You know, I don't know any females who wouldn't like to go and have a good role in the hay . . .

ROSS: Nor do I, they all like Bond.

LYNN: . . . get into the sack with Bond, but nobody would mention it afterwards. And this is the one security you would have with Bond, nobody would find out about it, unless some other little spy came in.

BRAD: Unless they read the book.

ROSS: I go along with part of what Lynn is saying here, because I feel that the ladies who had a little adventure with this mythical man, this Bond . . . shall we be very Sherlock Holmsian in this. When they had had it, they were well loved, but they never went around bragging about it, so obviously, there was a little bit of respect, give and take, but a bit of respect. Because Bond also never went around opening his yap that he'd been into the Queen of the May or this or that.

INTERVIEWER I: No, he was rather discreet about it. He said "she was a nice girl."

ROSS: He was, he was a real gentleman. I think what he brought was a bit of respectability to the art of wenching, which is going out of style. For Chrisake, it really is, You go up now, and try to be nice to a woman, and she thinks you're square.

MARJORIE: Just because he didn't kiss and tell . . .

ROSS: I think that men can find in Bond a little bit of the way they would like to be received by a lady. I think there's a hell of a lot of this in all his books.

LYNN: And I feel from a female point of view, that

I wouldn't mind at all meeting somebody like Bond. You could have a nice time with him and nobody'd ever know about it.

CAROL: And I think most females feel this way.

ROSS: You'd be well protected, too, you know, in case anybody came crashing in through the door.

LYNN: Yes, I'd have M. I. 5 or whatever behind me.

INTERVIEWER I: We have a problem — You see, I've been very lazy and not taking any notes, and we're talking over each other.

LYNN: Do you think I would have spoken if you'd been taking notes.

CAROL: About the people who read these books. I feel the men do associate themselves with James Bond very definitely. The women, I think I'd break down into two groups . . . the kind that are James Bond Girl types, and say, "I haven't met a man like that in a long time,"

BOB: Or ever.

CAROL: Well, maybe not or ever. And then also the sweet innocent little type, who thinks, well one of these days, James Bond is going to give it all up. He's going to settle down and marry, and I'm going to be there.

INTERVIEWER: Miss Moneypenny.

INTERVIEWER II: I want to ask Lynn something on her last point. Would you appreciate the man who is not terribly debonair? . . . who would not take you to the finest restaurant in town, and order all the right liquors, but would take you to an offbeat little place where they serve good food and good wine, and he is basically a poet, not an adventurer. Could you go for that?

LYNN: Well, you stop me right there when you say a poet . . . I don't go for poets at all.

. . . LAUGHTER . . . Well, if it is a good restaurant where they serve good food and good wine, fine.

INTERVIEWER: I was thinking more of the man than the restaurant. In other words, he's a poet. He perhaps wouldn't know the correct wine to order with the meal.

LYNN: Well, if he didn't know the correct wine to order, I wouldn't be out with him in the first place. And I might add if he didn't know the correct wine, I'd be there to correct him.
(LAUGHTER) I just defeated myself, didn't I.
ROSS: There's just a little bit of give and take, isn't there.
INTERVIEWER: John, you're definitely a Bond fan, do you agree that he's probably every man's dream?
JOHN: Well I think most of my opinions have all been expressed during the back and forth discussion. I don't think there's anything that vague or complex about Bond. He is the old fashioned super-hero. About the criticisms of him, he's neither stupid, nor a boor, nor a snob. He's extremely cultured . . . and intelligent. He has a university education as you can tell from reading his books. The super hero goes back to God. God is the original super hero. If you have a person who cannot be faulted in any way, who can never lose, who is the one creature-entity who is above all things, then you get mass appeal — that's God — that's Superman. Superman is the outstanding comic strip hero because bullets don't hurt him, he can fly.
MAJORIE: He's omnipotent.
BOB: Fairies fly, too.
JOHN: Bond is the same kind of super hero. He always comes out in the end. And the criticism about his being pro-English all the time. I don't think he's a snob that way. He always goes to another country. In every book, he's in a different country, and the villains are usually indigenous to that country. There is though, in Bond, a very strong anti-ethnic streak. He points out what's wrong with the Japanese. The Japanese stubborness and narrow-mindedness and their love for suicide. He points out the stupidity of the Filipino and he points out the dullness of the French, and their stupid mistakes.

BOB: Isn't that the author?

LYNN: One step beyond the author.

JOHN: Well of course it's the author — but the point is — about the hero he's always in a different country, and the enemy is always in a different country, and he points out these characteristics — but he always has great respect for his enemy. SMERSH is an intelligent, highly complex, very well organized machine and in the same way that Bond's people have number 1's and number 2's and number 3's — so does SMERSH. The enemy in one of his books has widow's pensions for the families of people who die.

INTERVIEWER I: Benevolent villains.

ROSS: I don't think that Fleming, when he was writing these books ever thought that they'd be analysed so well as they're being done here now. I don't think, John, that this has any bearing on his books. For the simple reason that Fleming was a guy who wrote a book which became a best seller, and he kept on writing it.

LYNN: Why does anybody have to analyse "why?" Why?

INTERVIEWER I: Because it's commercial and the publisher is paying for it.

MARJORIE: Nobody's analysed anything but his appeal.

BOB: Nobody's concerned about the fact that Bond has a license to kill. All that people seem to be concerned about is his bedroom prowess — and his grace at the table.

ROSS: But isn't the point of the exercise to know what sort of man was Fleming, that wrote these books. Not what his books are, his books are there, Fleming isn't.

LYNN: Did you know that about three years ago, there was a James Bond Club in Toronto, made up mainly of lawyers?

JOHN: Universal Export, that's right. They had their meetings, and they drank his drinks and ate his food,

BOB: And what did they do to his women?
ROSS: I was going to ask the same thing.
LYNN: I'm not about to tell.
JOHN: Ian Fleming was quoted as saying that he wrote the Bond books just for fun.
MARJORIE: I don't believe that.
BOB: And you read them for fun.
MARJORIE: Everybody takes exception to that, his biographers, his friends.
JOHN: I don't agree with that at all.
MARJORIE: You take his last book — in particular ... the one that's set in Japan — he didn't write them for fun.
LYNN: He *did*.
You know one of these days we're going to be setting here talking about your books (the interviewer's) and we're going to say — he didn't write them for fun, he wrote them for money.
BRAD: James Bond — Ian Fleming lived in Jamaica. There's a guy there ... what Bond writes about in his books is not entirely fiction. We met a guy there. He's a Jamaican who is more colourful than Dr. No. He's probably between 70 and 80 years old, very wealthy, owns a string of brothels, nightclubs and grocery stores.
JOHN: A lot of strings.
LYNN: Something for everybody.
BRAD: I'm coming to the best string. He has a different wife every year.
BOB: I can relate to that guy.
BRAD: This is far more intriguing than most fiction. And you have never seen such beautiful women in your life. When they get to be twenty, they're too old, and he ships them back to Hong Kong and gets a new one
BOB: What's the depreciation on one of those?
MARJORIE: What's this got to do with the Secret Service.
BRAD: When I talked about this guy — everybody was silent. You were interested. When you tell a story —

you embroider it a bit —
LYNN: Poetic license.
BRAD: The same thing with Ian Fleming — it was your Mr. Maugham who said "He's only a story teller, and he happens to be good at it." In being a story teller, Ian Fleming has altered the facts a bit. He has come across so many situations that are interesting to so many people, and he's gotten the books out. And his books have been most entertaining. He has excellent taste as to what makes good copy and what doesn't. I know 50 million editors at the Star, Telegram and Canadian Press who don't have this taste. He had it, and became very successful as a result. He recreated the romantic man of the Renaissance who could do anything.
JOHN: I don't think he's romantic at all. He's an exciting hero . . .
ROSS: He didn't sit down to write a best seller, he sat down to write a book, and it suddenly caught on.
BRAD: This guy does everything well, that's why I say he's romantic. The sex is negligible — His books aren't sexy.
BOB: It's a bunch of asterisks.
BRAD: It's not erotic writing.
MARJORIE: Yes, Granted.
BRAD: It's his adventure.
JOHN: I don't grant that at all.
As soon as anyone mentions the name James Bond, the first thing most people think of is the women in James Bond's books. The thing about the movies is the gorgeous women.
BRAD: You're talking about the movies, not the books.
JOHN: I am very definitely talking about the books, because the movies were based on the books . . . the only thing the movies had that was different was a few more gimmicks. They had the same plot, the same character outline, the same idea . . . the same thing.
MARJORIE: And a lot more time devoted to the

women.

INTERVIEWER II: Weren't the movies really the director's concept, not Ian Fleming's?

BOB: They had a lot more bedroom time.

EDNA: May I introduce something that is completely different. I'm going to sound terribly suburban and terribly square — but really I'm not a James Bond fan, and one of the things that irks me about it,

BRAD: Is it that your husband tries to act like him?

EDNA: (continues) My kids think that James Bond is the greatest, the most marvellous because he can kill anyone. The kids on the street where we live think it's great . . . if they hear somebody died they want to know who shot him. This is what I have against Bond. The whole thing has become so darned commercial, where youngsters of five, six and seven have as their greatest hero a James Bond who can kill — a killer. And they don't know about the sex part.

BRAD: That figures.

BOB: What about Roy Rogers?

LYNN: He sings you to death

ROSS: Are these little boys or girls?

EDNA: They're boys, and they'd like to kill the girls. Roy Rogers only killed bad guys.

ROSS: Always little boys like the killing business.

BOB: And the messier the better.

ROSS: In the days of the great British Empire — it's long ago now, little boys were fighting the Battle of Inkerman.

EDNA: It disturbs me.

LYNN: James Bond operates within the framework of the secret service. As far as the secret service in the Bond books is concerned, it's reasonably authentic, at least I have it on fairly good authority that his secret service bits are reasonably authentic . . . so I don't see that you can quarrel with this, I see that you can quarrel with *his* characteristics.

INTERVIEWER II: I want to throw one question at you . . . I hope you won't throw your glasses at me. I want to suggest that Fleming, in writing Bond, was looking for outlet . . . looking for escape . . . I want to suggest that Fleming, the man who had been terribly mother-ridden and was then terribly wife ridden, was trying to express himself as a man, saying, My God, I'm really a man, I'm an adventurer . . . and this is why he wrote Bond.

ROSS: I think this is highly possible.

MARJORIE: You've just said he wrote it for fun.

ROSS: You can still write for fun, but this is a different thought.

JOHN: Isn't that a marvellous way to have fun. To put down in print everything that you want to be.

ROSS: Fleming probably didn't know that he was writing to express himself.

INTERVIEWER II: If he was terribly repressed — all his life —

ROSS: Bond didn't know — the fact is that he didn't know that he was writing something that would be a best seller.

MARJORIE: How do you account for the fact that Fleming's life emulates Bond's books (sic).

JOHN: It doesn't. That's publicity and propaganda.

MARJORIE: It does, to a certain extent.

LYNN: I still say that I don't think anybody that repressed could write Bond.

INTERVIEWER II: I wonder if the repressed man doesn't become the great fantasy man?

MARJORIE: Well, who else could write it?

CAROL: If Ian Fleming were sitting here and listening to this, he'd —

BOB: He'd leave. He'd be insulted

CAROL: He really would.

LYNN: I don't think that Bond was that repressed —

INTERVIEWER: *FLEMING.*

LYNN: Fleming, I think that Fleming to write this

sort of thing would have to be a little more open, and in life.

ROSS: Fleming had a rather strange childhood —

BOB: Who didn't?

BRAD: I had, too.

ROSS (continues) where he was brought up in Edwardian elegance, lots of money, he was farmed out here, and farmed out there.

INTERVIEWER: Had no father after age of eight.

ROSS: Where he was — I don't know the American word, but the British word is "buggered" when he was at school, and it became the normal practice, and he had the turn of the new boys, and everything. In other words, he became a healthy product of the English Public School System. I say that if you've had your jollies that way, that it's going to have some effect on you some other way. He went on — he had always had money during his life, except when he went out one or two times on his own, and he was a bit short of cash, but he always bounced back and his big break was being with Reuters when he was in Moscow.

INTERVIEWER: And his mother got him the job.

ROSS: That's right, and he did well from there on. Coming around now to your question, I think that a lot of what he'd had in his past — the elegant life, and took that as the normal standard — I do not think that he has given Jimmie Bond (007) any heterosexual (sic) ideas or anything like that I think that he felt that love and life was a plain healthy way, and I think this is what he gave to Bond.

MARJORIE: What about the Japanese book — "You Only Live Twice" where Bond has been drinking, Bond is dispirited, Bond doesn't see any future for himself, in anything. He doesn't see much purpose to the Secret Service.

BRAD: Happens to everybody.

MARJORIE: Will you wait a minute. Muggeridge says

when he read the book, he thought Fleming was at the end of his tether, and what happens after the book? Fleming dies.
JOHN: No he wrote three other books after that.
MARJORIE: No he didn't.
ROSS: The Man With the Golden Gun was written after that.
LYNN: The Man With the Golden Gun wasn't written by him. When he died, there was an announcement that he had outlined the plot of a story. A few months later he had almost finished it, and still later "He had completed it."
MARJORIE: Anyway, it was published posthumously.
JOHN: I am convinced that is beautiful propaganda and press releases
LYNN: The Man With the Golden Gun has nothing to do with James Bond or Ian Fleming.
MARJORIE: This isn't press releases, this is Kingsley Amis, who wrote the book "James Bond Dossier," who knew him, who was his friend.
JOHN: James Bond stories, we must remember, came into popularity about three months after a story quoted John F. Kennedy as saying he liked them.
MARJORIE: That was here!
JOHN: Yes, and it was over there too, because these books were written in the fifties. James Bond was not as popular in England as a writer of mystery stories, as Eric Ambler was.
MARJORIE: He didn't write as much.
JOHN: Right, but I'm trying to say that this whole Bond phenomenon came about after Kennedy's statement.
ROSS: This is true and Fleming admits it.
CAM: From an employment point of view, maybe my job, I find Bond very interesting.
MARJORIE: His geography is very inaccurate, is that what you were going to say?

CAM: His geography is tremendously accurate. I'm a student in geography

MARJORIE: All sorts of people say his Thrilling Cities is bad, bad, bad.

CAM: Secondly, Bond with his experience in the Secret Service, letting little things drop along the line. We've learned something from him. There have been other TV things like Danger Man, Man from Uncle — they're fantastic. These things actually happened.

MARJORIE: I don't think anyone here has quarrelled with the Secret Service aspect.

CAM: Now Bond taught us one thing — you can take a book from the point of view of geography, of sex, of adventure, or you can take it from pure fact, or you can take it from a release of mind, whatever you want. Everyone takes a book in different ways. I took out of Bond what I wanted and that was all these remarkable inventions. They were fantastic.

BRAD: I didn't read into Bond the women — the sex. I said "Ah fine, you know, he's with this dizzy broad — that'll be over in a while — we'll get back to the business.

MARJORIE: What did you see in it?

BRAD: The adventure. And the gimmicks, the little facts. Quite frankly, he impressed me. Well, he's in a dining room in Casino Royale . . . baccarat.

LYNN: I love gambling, and I admire his prowess.

BRAD: They don't play baccarat in North America — well, they didn't until Casino Royale, 1953. Bond — or Fleming has more influence on our society than I think Ian Fleming would have wanted. If somebody said to me, Brad, write a book, and I could cause the kind of stir that this man did — with the result, that Edna says her kids worship Bond — I wouldn't want that kind of responsibility, so that all the world says I want to be like Brad Ferris. Boy, it frightens me . . . I would be writing to entertain my friends . . . my God, I'd feel like God. He was writing to entertain.

BOB: Talk about Bond — it was one long ruddy commercial.
BRAD: He took a character who actually lived in Jamaica and he made him Dr. No. Dr. No lived on an island covered with bird-shit.
EDNA: That's right, that's how he died, isn't it?
BOB: He was buried under tons of bird-shit.
BRAD: I always thought this was kind of funny. It seems like a just reward for a guy who is a bad fellow.
LYNN: Why is there more fuss about the violence in James Bond than in Mickey Spillane? What's the difference?
MARJORIE: Well, they were operating at a different class level, but what's the difference?
JOHN: There was just as wide a Mickey Spillane cult as there is a Bond cult.
MARJORIE: You mean products and everything?
JOHN: Sure, there was a Mickey Spillane gun and Mickey Spillane kit.
CONNIE: Mickey Spillane was Mike Hammer, wasn't he? Well, he was all bad, there wasn't any good in him.
MARJORIE: I didn't think Mike Hammer was all bad, at all.
JOHN: They had this one thing in common. They were heroes, and they had all kinds of women, and they each had flaws in their character. And this makes them almost human
MARJORIE: Couldn't they have virtues?
JOHN: They did have virtues.
BRAD: Many of them.
MARJORIE: Like knowing what kind of wine to order, or how to play bridge — or
JOHN: Knowing how to treat a woman.
MARJORIE: What do you mean, knowing how to treat a woman?
JOHN: No, I don't mean how to lay a woman — how to treat her, how to talk to her, to walk with her, to give

her comfort.
BRAD: Very gentle.
MARJORIE: I've never heard him talk!
INTERVIEWER: But do you think Bond gave comfort to women?
JOHN: Oh yes, that poor pathetic little creature that he married ...
BRAD: And he was charitable.
INTERVIEWER I: But he got rid of her, he killed her off .... or she was killed off, fortunately ...
JOHN: But he fell in love with many of the women in the books. He fell in love with the girl in From Russia With Love.
MARJORIE: Maybe he was just rationalizing his sex.
BOB: How was the trip on the Mayflower?
JOHN: What amuses me is all this great discussion about this, and it's not worth having, it's not great art, it's not great literature, it's amusing, pleasant little happenstance, it's a piece of fluff.
MARJORIE: Why else do you have to fall in love with somebody, other than to justify your —
BRAD: Alright, what virtues would you ascribe to your conception of the perfect man?
MARJORIE: I haven't got any conception of the perfect man — I would take you or you or you as you come. Or not take you.
JOHN: Bond is not perfect. The one thing that we haven't pointed out is that Bond is very stupid, he invariably makes mistakes. He invariably gets caught. He always gets caught by the enemy. And at the last minute he's remembering that idiotic thing he shouldn't have done.
BOB: But he triumphs.
BRAD: Marjorie — what is a good man, what virtues do you see in a good man?
MARJORIE: What I don't see is superficiality.
BRAD: What do you see?

MARJORIE: I'm not on trial.

BRAD: No, but I'm trying to defend poor old James Bond. I like him.

MEANWHILE JOHN HAS CONTINUED ON THE BOND FORMULA

JOHN: You see, in each book the formula is standard. He comes on, usually remembering something from the last book, point 1. Then comes the great respect for M, point 2. You see M as the father figure, and Bond as the one person M has respect for. Then, there's a little reference to show that in between running after spies and women, Bond does office work. Then comes the journey to a faraway land, Japan, China, India, so on. Then comes this crazy plot, and it's always something very far fetched, like atomic bombs that have been stolen, breaking into unbreakable banks.

INTERVIEWER I: John what about James Bond's gambling? Is this something that appeals to you?

JOHN: No, that didn't appeal to me particularly, but you see, gambling puts him with high society, it's the environment of the gambling — always in the posh clubs.

BOB: A lot of men like to gamble, but don't because they can't afford to, or are bad gamblers.

BRAD: No, but I'm trying to defend poor old James

JOHN: But you see in each book, you get Bond being adept at a different art. He's a brilliant skier in one, he knows all the tricks about skiing; he plays a brilliant game of golf in another, he knows all the ins and outs of the game.

BOB: Remember, he smashed Goldfinger at golf.

JOHN: And there's the card game, the baccarat game ... and he's an expert at bridge. In each book, there's a different facility he has where he's absolutely brilliant.

LYNN: As we'd all like to be.

JOHN: And I found those the dullest chapters of all, because I thought "He's writing this to show how much

he knows about this game, or this sport."
BOB: The author has researched it and there it is in print.
INTERVIEWER I: It was interesting to read the biographies of Fleming, and to see Fleming's comment as to why he so thoroughly documented his books. What about all this extraneous detail? He said the more detailed you make information about food and drinks and activities and whatever, the more believable these far out plots become.
BOB: I don't agree with that. Because it's unbelievable that people would walk around speaking in brand names.
JOHN: That's something to relate to, that's something to know. If he had written a book about Toronto, where he described driving down Yonge Street, just past St. Clair, at the subway, everybody in Toronto would notice. I've been in movies, where they flash a scene of Toronto, and everybody reacts. Even if Canada is mentioned in a movie. This is relating. Something you're familiar with.
BOB: Bond's descriptions — Fleming's descriptions of American scenes, and I've travelled quite a bit in the States, are not very realistic. For instance his Miami bits, are not the Miami I know. His New York bits aren't the New York that I know from having been there, and I know New York very well. He creates something that is germane to his writing, germane to the plot of his novel, convenient. For example the CIA men in a couple of his books are Fleming's CIA men. Real CIA men ain't like that.
CONNIE: How many CIA men have you ever met?
BOB: Let's face reality . . . "The Spy Who Came In From the Cold" is more of a spy than the spies in the Bond books.
JOHN: The thing that amuses me most of all is all these great detailed studies. I really think that Fleming,

in the time that he was alive, would have thought this whole thing ridiculous. He thought why not write a best-seller.

BOB: I don't think he said, "Why not write a best-seller? I think he said why not write a book, and I can make some money out of it."

JOHN: And you see, shortly after Kennedy made his announcement, Fleming wrote three or four of them, and they came up like mad.

BOB: You know where I've read most of my James Bond books?

BRAD: In bed.

BOB: No, as a matter of fact not in bed, on a plane going somewhere on a business trip.

INTERVIEWER I: That's what Fleming said. He was writing for all the people in berths on trains, on ships, on planes, and getting them to turn the next page.

BOB: I'm going on a business trip to New York, or Montreal, or whatever, and I'm reading a James Bond book, because to me travel's now become dull. I'm fed up. I get tired of this business of an hour and a half to New York, or an hour to Montreal, so you read a book, now this makes the flight pass easier, and when you've arrived, you've almost finished the book, so you finish it that night in the hotel, or something. And you think Gee, I'm in Montreal, and whoopsie, am I going to swing in Montreal. And you come off that plane, all full of James Bond vim, vigor and vitality, and you go to the hotel, have a drink and you go to bed, This is reality, not Bond books — that's not reality.

JOHN: Some day I'll take you to Montreal.

INTERVIEWER I: Are the James Bond women feminine? You boys are fans, are those women feminine?

BOB: Feminine women? Oh boy!

INTERVIEWER II: Not the exterior shell, but is there a woman inside the shell?

BOB: No they're not feminine, it's the body, just the

body. Apertures, a leg in each corner, a head on top — the usual equipment.

INTERVIEWER II: Nothing inside?

BOB: Just some vital organs, perhaps, but that's not germane.

BRAD: No, you can't get too far inside, because you paint them all gold when you're finished in three pages.

BOB: They're not real women, because women like that don't exist. Women have faults, they're not all gorgeously perfect.

INTERVIEWER II: Are these women perfect?

BOB: No, it's fancy masturbation.

JOHN: I would say the women are as real as James Bond is. It's the whole character. The whole James Bond image, as I said in my first statement is the superhero, it's as good and as great and as marvellous and exciting as you can get. And you can't top that.

BOB: You know that James Bond, in every book, after you've read a book or two, you know that he's going to get caught in some improbable trap, he's going to be staked out in the sun for the ants to eat his private parts or something, and he's going to escape.

BRAD: At the last minute, though. It's a formula, really,

BOB: And his villains all die in a violent, peculiar manner. Dr. No gets buried under tons of bird dung.

INTERVIEWER I: What about Kress who the villain gets fed the fish. As he is sleeping, somebody shoves a fish into his mouth. Symbolic, I thought.

BRAD: That was in a short story, and that was a classic short story that Bond had written. Did you hear about that? That was a terrible thing. It was like a sun fish, you know, and Bond wasn't in this.

JOHN: That was the book I found dullest of all.

BOB: Terrific!

BRAD: How do you kill a guy, you know, this guy's a real nut ... he's got a big yacht, and he's beating the government for taxes, so some broad grabs a fish, and

scrambles him with it. Boom, right in his yap. If you pull it out, the fins gotta stick. Oh that's a great way.
EDNA: What!
BRAD: It's a sunfish, you see
BOB: And it's got spines on it.
BRAD: And you know how it blows up with UGH!
BOB: Have you ever been fishing, and caught a sunfish with the big needles on it?
BRAD: You can only grab him by his head and pull back, you can't pull him from his tail and pull up.
BOB: They've got spines in them, they'll tear your hand off.
BRAD: So this person grabs — this guy is a millionaire who has a yacht and he is a real bad fellow, twenty pages have been devoted to proving how bad a guy he is, so they grab him by the nose, and they say, have one of your famous sunfish — he's a tropical fish catcher, and they've got this rare fish with fins that go under, and this person rams the fish in his yap, and it gags him, you see, right down his throat — and he can't pull it out, oh, it's horrible you see —
BOB: The spines dig into the roof of his mouth,
BRAD: But it's justice — it prevails.
EDNA: This is entertainment?
BOB: No his villains are all very villainous, extremely villainous, and they meet foul ends.
BRAD: Bad villains. They don't even give to the Salvation Army.
INTERVIEWER II: Speaking of villains, what was this bit where they stuck Bond on top of a pipe which was going to erupt with eight million tons of hot mud?
BRAD: The world's biggest enema. This is the guy he buried in bird shit.
BOB: He had it coming to him.
JOHN: That seems fair — turnabout.
BRAD: It's only justice. I don't really think that Bond is anything that is taken seriously, there's no message

there, it's just that it's like . . .

BOB: The flight's arrived in Montreal — time to close the book, and head for the limousine.

BRAD: Like a cartoon, you watch it, it's over, okay what's on next?

BOB: You know the whole society has a preoccupation with violence. I have a child who will be four years old in another week or so, and if he hasn't got an object in his hand to make a gun — It could be a fork — one day he picked up his foot and shot me with his foot. Does this mean that this kid is going to be a murderer?

INTERVIEWER II: No, he's going to grow up to be a North American male.

JOHN: He's got four strange feet.

BOB: His big toe expectorates.

JOHN: When you pull it back, his big toe goes click!

BOB: But the point of this, is he's not perverting and destroying contemporary society,

JOHN: The whole thing is so amusing, all these great studies and all these books that have been written and are going to be written, on why this happens, the Bond thing.

BRAD: Who's laughing more than Fleming was.

JOHN: I think the outstanding example is the Mickey Spillane thing. When you see how popular Mickey Spillane was, and the movies they made, and the television series, and the whole thing, was the same cycle. It faded away, he got religion, or something.

CONNIE: Well, he stopped writing, and Fleming died.

BOB: He used to have his heroines, for example — One of his favorite gimmicks was to take a 45 automatic, which is a particularly repulsive type of gun — a cannon — well it's a half inch bullet, 45 calibre, and he'd put it against the navel of his heroine, and pull the trigger. Now that goes SPLAT.

BRAD: And comes out like that (gesturing) on the other side.

BOB: This is the Spillane type of violence.
JOHN: I wonder whatever happened to Lewis Carrol.
BRAD: Spillane got him. Right in the navel.

CHAPTER IX

What It Was All About

In examining James Bond, the Bond Cult, and Ian Fleming, the man who was responsible for it all, it's important to remain objective, questioning and noncritical. A hatchet job on Bond or Bond's creator wouldn't bring any insight into the fascinating unconscious meanings of the whole thing. A full length apology for Fleming and Bond wouldn't be very interesting — since adulation and hero worship, untempered by a glimpse of the feet of clay, make bland fare.

The Bond books, say qualified experts in psychology and psychiatry, are a kind of instinctual riot. They offer Bond fans the opportunity to act out their most cherished fantasies. Bond belongs to a fantasy life, not to reality. His creation and his adventures are a successful attempt to deny reality, to deny the frustrations and limitations of every day living.

For Bond fans, and perhaps for Ian Fleming, Bond was the opportunity to deny weakness. Fleming created Bond, he said, to relieve the hysteria created by his precipitous marriage at 43. Many men feel before or after they marry, that they are small boys, back in the grip of their mothers. Something from way back in the past seems to be reasserting itself . . . they are weak . . . and once again, however temporarily, in the control of a woman.

For Fleming, being deprived of his father at the age of eight was a traumatic experience. The father, after all, is of tremendous importance in assisting a young boy to gain a masculine identification, and to cope with all the feelings he has of being entwined by his mother.

Clearly, Fleming, as a sensitive product of his early environment identified with Bond in a grandiose way. Bond really has supernatural powers, and narcissistic self love enforces masculinity in an attempt to cling to fantasies of power from early childhood. Such fantasies are especially characteristic of a five to six year old boy, and maybe manifested in a fasincation or preoccupation with guns.

This same type of fantasy, frequently repeated in adolescence, is manifested in a preoccupation with cars — big long cars.

In short, it's a fantasy of hypermasculinity comparable to "red-blooded American male" fantasy, acted out in so many American movies. John Wayne, for instance, the epitome of the cruelly masculine red-blooded American male lives out the fantasy, in his own life — he has become well known as a right-wing political extremist.

Men who spend their lives acting out the fantasy of masculinity have a great need to repress their own femininity, weakness, passivity, say the experts. Like the Nazis, they must engage in a glorification of power and violence, and a strong denial of weakness, femininity, or feminine identification. The fact of the denial, is usually an indication that at some level, there is strong feminine identification. Worship of exacting physical achievement, great dedication to excellence at sports, often goes along with this denial.

A more mature state of self, say psychoanalysts, would give recognition to both masculine and feminine aspects of the personality, and allow them to exist in harmony together, rather than in conflict.

It's true, comment the experts, that the Bond books seem to glorify power and sadism . . . a sadism unmodified by gentler attitudes. Throughout the adventures of Double O Seven, there are repeated references to kicking, bruising, chewing, beating and mangling various parts of the body. The tortures inflicted on Bond threaten castration, the most terrible fate of all.

The fantasy of power, say doctors, is very much bound up with an attempt to deny fears of castration, and to experience them actively, rather than passively.

In Live and Let Die, for instance, there is clear expression of oral sadism. Mr. Big has Bond and Solitaire bloodied first, then tied to the back of a power boat, to be dragged through shark-infested waters. The whole fantasy involved, obviously, is of a person being bitten to pieces and swallowed, in short, a particularly horrifying type of oral castration.

In fantasy, dominating mothers swallow up their sons. There might also be, say analysts, a projection onto the mother, of wishes to bite the breast. At that age, the infant and young child projects his own fantasies on to the mother, so that if he felt very frustrated during this period, he would project onto his mother, the fantasies of being eaten alive.

Erickson has written of the Sioux Indians, a particularly cruel and ferocious tribe, that they go through an extremely frustrating period from the age of about six months to eighteen months, where they are bound in very tightly, and pulled roughly from the breast after a short feeding. This, of course, gives rise to tremendous frustration, aggression and hostility. No wonder the Sioux are so fierce.

Ask an avid Bond fan what he likes about the books, and be struck at once by the great free play of fantasy, the fantasy gratification which explains the success of Fleming's writing formula. The formula which effectively denies reality.

Bond possesses all superhuman powers, and many ordinary people, perhaps with Fleming himself, have a great need for this. In Bond, with his license to kill, the conscience is denied. He is allowed to act out murderous wishes, in a kind of anesthetization of the conscience, allowing free play to destructive fantasies. This can bring a great deal of gratification to the ordinary guy who has had a hard day at the office.

That man, all tensed up and reading the Bond books, can finally go to bed feeling quite relaxed, having acted it all out through the Superhero's adventures.

The Bond reader can, in this way, dispose of his hated boss, or the nagging wife, or seduce that sexy looking girl in the next office — all without punishment, all without permanent involvement.

In the early Bond books, there were occasional mentions of Bond's conscience. He didn't like then, to kill in what he called "cold blood." Later, toward the end of the series, Bond didn't mind killing nearly so much. It was something that had to be done, and he was there to do it.

Anne Fleming said that, in creating Bond, her late husband had made a kind of Frankenstein's monster which eventually took him over.

It may be, say the experts, that after Fleming's marriage, his need to act out his killing fantasies grew much greater, either because of what his wife meant in terms of his fantasied relationship to his mother, or in terms of what she was realistically (overpowering, if we can believe descriptions from her friends).

Male members of the Bond cult, then, gain satisfaction from acting out their own fantasies and aggressions. The women who step from the pages of the Bond-books sometimes seem to be phallic-masculine types, which might suggest Fleming's and Bond's fears of such women, yet fatal fascination with them.

Nearly every Bond girl favors a wide leather belt. Is this indicative of a fetish, we wondered. Analysts explained that any fetish represents a phallus, or penis, in a woman. A little boy both fears that a woman might have a penis, and that she might not. Because if she doesn't, then he might lose his.

Far less complicated, and much easier to understand are Bond's sexual adventures. The Bond girls are not true sexual objects, and the adventures are not true object relationships, they're a series of love 'em and leave 'em episodes. He avoids involvement and wields complete power over the women and the relationships. If you permit yourself to become involved, you're enmeshed and castrated, and you lose your identity. That's how the experts describe the Don Juan syndrome exhibited by Bond.

Occasionally Fleming permitted Bond to flirt with involvement, but he was always freed in the end. If he didn't extricate himself, Fleming, as the author, killed the girl off for him.

Examination of Fleming's work by experts in psychoanalysis, indicate that perhaps he, like a lot of other people, never overcame the symbiotic stage with the mother. When a child is very little, he feels, not like a separate person from the mother, but rather, instead, as though they are interlinked. This gives rise to all kinds of problems, and in the most serious manifestations of symbiosis, fears of the woman may be too great to permit marriage.

Critics frequently dismissed Bond as smacking of sex, sadism and snobbery. Envy of a glamorous kind of life is an extremely common psycho-analytic theme. It turns up, say the experts, in almost every patient in psychoanalysis. The glamorous, jet-set life really represents the private sexual life of the parents, from which the child is excluded. Often, the life of the jet set is tremendously glamorized, and the average person feels that he or she isn't good enough, and is for that reason excluded. The glamor of Bond, his flying visits to romantic, far-off countries, his meals in the exotic restaurants, and his knowledge of the right wines, all provide a respectable outlet for the childish fantasy of exclusion from the parent's sexual life.

Many, many people, say the experts, carry into adult life a recollection of seeing their parents go out, all dressed up, on what the children felt, was a tremendously glamorous occasion in which they had no part. This can carry, throughout life, a feeling of inadequacy and exclusion, which can be overcome only by attaining membership in a glamourous circle.

On the subject of brutality toward women — as evidenced by the description of Kerim's brutality to his gypsy captive, the experts agree it can be considered an immature form of sexuality, in which a man must demonstrate his power over a woman, in order to reassure himself of his potency.

It is also interesting to note that in almost every Bond book, where Bond and the current Bond girl are making love, the agent seizes the girl by her long hair. There are, say the professionals, strong phallic implications in that, too.

In every one of Ian Fleming's books, the superhero, Bond, is omnipotent — the far extreme opposite of impotence, say psychiatrists. This may be an attempt to recover childhood omnipotence which exists first, during the years from three to five, and is repeated later, at puberty.

It might also be an attempt to deny the aging process, the realization by a middle-aged man that life will no longer hold all the hopes he had enjoyed as a young man. By taking refuge in such narcissistic types of fantasy as total omnipotence, he can deny harsh reality.

In Casino Royale, the first of the Bond books, the hero actually reflects on fears about his potency. He has been so battered and beaten that he has serious doubts about whether he can perform satisfactorily sexually.

Bond frequently receives severe beatings at the hands

of the Bond villains, but always comes through in the end. In one story, he is worked over by two gangsters who don football spikes to do the job. In Live and Let Die, he receives terrible battering on a coral reef.

The symbolic use of spikes, say some analysts, justifies the belief that there is some connection between such tortures and fantasies of sadistic intercourse.

From the viewpoint of a psychoanalyst, the Bond stories are primitive, id level material, buried deep in the unconscious. They are like some of the downtown movie houses, where triple features of a gory type are screened continuously, and advertised in lurid posters outside.

That touch of elegance in Fleming's work, probably the result of his upbringing in an ultra-comfortable Edwardian home, raises the Adventures of James Bond a little above run-of-the-mill gore.

Did Fleming in his writing, make a conscious attempt to satisfy these dark interests and desires? Would a writer who so vividly recorded such chilling episodes realize what he was doing and why? The response of the experts was inconclusive, many writers, they said, have considerable insight into their work and themselves, others see themselves quite inaccurately.

The experts discussed available material on Fleming's childhood, his stay at Eton, his experiences with flogging, and his account of homosexual initiation which has been quoted so frequently.

To their knowledge, said the professionals, Eton, cannot be accurately described as "a tough school, which specialized in beating conformity into boys from the age of eight." Eton, they believed, has an atmosphere of more freedom than do many other English public schools.

The type of flogging described by Fleming's friends as having been endured by him is not common now, if indeed it ever was.

Nor, say the experts, is the homosexual initiation of a new boy inevitable. Common enough, perhaps, but not inevitable.

What is important, clearly, is that Fleming himself believed all these things to be true, pointing perhaps to a strong indication of bisexuality.

Not, the psychiatrists emphasized, what the layman understands by bisexuality. To the average person, bisexuality means acting out both masculine forms of sexuality or heterosexuality, and homosexuality.

Bisexuality, to the experts, means a preoccupation with and insecurity about one's maleness, and a lot of feminine-type fantasies. That does not necessarily mean that these fantasies are always actually acted out, that the person involved is consciously, or openly homosexual.

Bond's world is a magical one. The remarkable inventions and gadgets which figure so prominently in the Bond books are of great interest to adolescent boys the age group 13 to 16, when they are greatly preoccupied with inventions. An adolescent boy in treatment, for instance, might go on for a long time talking about some marvellous invention and all its parts, indicating his own preoccupation with masculinity and the phallus. The invention, actually, is representative of the phallus. Bond's magic world of power and accompanying denial of all the limtiations of reality is the most marked feature of Fleming's works.

"M" appears in the Bond books, as the mock father figure, very powerful, very critical, and possibly even represents the father that Fleming lost and wanted. There is also the possibility, however, that the bad father is represented in the villain — the fantasy of the bad, enemy father who would take away the boy's mother.

In discussing the facts of Fleming's life, it was clear that no responsible psychiatrist or psychoanalyst would do more than speculate. It does appear, however, that Ian Fleming's own picture of his childhood was a rather sado-masochistic one, probably to a greater extent than could be justified by reality. Perhaps, out of his own nature, he was inclined to dramatize some rather ordinary experiences. A lot of people go through life doing just that. The really important thing is not what actually happened, what experiences they actually endured, but the way in which they recall them and interpret them and are worried or fearful or ashamed of them.

Much has been said, some of it snide, some of it speculative, about Ian Fleming's authorship of The Spy Who Loved Me. The book, written in the first person female, was an account by the heroine, Vivienne Michel of her terror at the hands of two small-time American gangsters, her story-book rescue by James Bond, who just happened to be passing by, and her passionately gratifying love episode with the same James Bond.

How, raged, the critics, desperately trying to enforce their own masculinity, could any normal man write a book in the first person female, and then, mindful of the implications, try to cover his tracks by penning a coy introduction, which caroled that Miss Michel had left the manuscript on his desk.

Was the author who produced such a product a homosexual, or a transvestite? What did it all mean.

Probably nothing very significant, say the experts. Perhaps only that Fleming the author had tired of the same old formula, and decided to try his hand at a new one. When he saw the results of his attempt, he decided not to argue with success, and reverted to the proven pattern.

All the probing, and digging, and analysing in the world can't change one thing. Ian Fleming, whatever his background, and whatever his neuroses and whatever his reasons, hit on a formula which captured the imagination of millions of readers.

No matter what the experts and the critics and the

Carrie Nations of the literary world think or say or do, those millions of fans will go on enjoying the Bond books, and mourning the fact that there will be no more.

CHAPTER X

The Legacy of the Golden Pen

Many things may be disputed about Fleming — Bond, but one thing is clear. Ian Fleming made a remarkable impact on the reading habits of millions all over the world.

People who almost never read, became voracious readers of the exploits of James Bond. Others, who read only what they would term "serious things," became avid fans of 007. And why not?

Bond's sexploits provided many men whose mundane lives chained them to uninteresting suburban housewives with curlers in their hair with a chance to live an exciting daydream. Through the easily read pages of Fleming's books, they lived vicariously in a world of violence, glamor and beautiful women. Ah, the women.

No frumpy housewives here, not in the world of Bond. By merely turning the pages of a book, the man without a dream (or a very satisfactory sex life either) travelled as Bond through the world where all women are beautiful, sexy, uninhibited and anxious to give their all to the man with sufficient daring to take it.

Men? But what about the female Bond fans? Ah yes, gentle reader, they too found their day dreams in the person of 007, and what day dreams they were.

While the male Bond fans drooled over the icy beauties who undulated through the pages, they also thrilled at their hero's cunning, daring, strength, and all the things that made 007 the superman he was.

The female fans, it seems, cared less about his ability to slay dragons than they did about his ability to lay fair damsels. Erotic imagery is not the sole property of the male. One beautiful, sophisticated admirer of bondage with Bond stated with disarming frankness that she "would just love to go for a roll in the hay with a real life James Bond."

A lot of women who wouldn't know a Bentley from a Beretta, do know a suave, sophisticated man such as James Bond from the slobs they married. They too lived vicariously and dreamed their dreams of giving their all to 007 at the zip of a zipper.

Here was the ultimate in escape for those who needed escape from a life of "two or three times a month with the lights out . . . No, George, not that way . . . That's up high enough, I don't have to take it right off . . . Those bloody curlers . . ."

But what now? When Fleming died, so did Bond. 007 can no more be resurrected than can Ian Fleming. The King is dead . . . Long live the King!

What of the millions who lived through Bond? Where do they go now? Back to suburbia? They can't. Having lifted the blue jean curtain and peeked at the exotic life of 007, they don't just want it, they need it.

And yet, whatever or whoever is going to fill this void has not yet appeared on the scene. Perhaps television comes closest.

Patrick MacNee in the Avengers provides the escape for many. So too, do the Men from UNCLE and a few others, but it isn't quite the same. In watching television, the man in search of a daydream must share the program with that dull woman with the curlers, with the kids who are fighting about three other programs they want to watch.

Worse, perhaps, the brief hour of glamorous escape must be interrupted by the strident voice of the announcer who tells why this pill is better for relieving stomach gas because it moves through your bowels faster and knows exactly where to go to bring relief. Who can daydream with a medicine man talking about stomach gas?

The little Bond book threw a fence around all the objectionable parts of the world and kept it out while the reader romped with tall, beautiful women who wore little but wide leather belts. Only a book has this power. But who will provide this dream world now?

Mickey Spillane? Doubtful. Sure, Mike Hammer tangles with beautiful women and has a gun and the power to kill, but that isn't enough. There remains some doubt that Hammer bathes frequently, he surely wouldn't know how to wear a tux, instead of ordering the correct wine, he is more likely to slug his whiskey straight from the bottle. In fact, there is a distinct possibility that he even picks his nose. Bond would have died rather than do that.

Somewhere today, the man who will take the place of 007 is perhaps emitting the squalling cries of birth. Perhaps some publisher has already slapped the baby's bottom to bring forth that first gasp of breath. Perhaps he is already strong and kicking up his heels but we just haven't noticed him yet. After all, we had Bond, we didn't need another.

On the other hand, perhaps there will be a continuance of the void. Perhaps only the next generation will find the perfect super hero. God knows, all indications point to their needing one to lend them a touch of exciting glamor.

But whatever happens, whether we loved, ignored or laughed at James Bond, he was here. We lived with a phenomenon and saw him die. A hell of a lot of people are going to miss him.

www.ingramcontent.com/pod-product-compliance
Lightning Source LLC
LaVergne TN
LVHW091259080426
835510LV00007B/324